STRENGTH&POWEREXERCISES
FORFIGHTERS

Over 30 Effective Exercises to Improve Strength & Power for Combat Athletes

JASON**CURTIS**

FUNDAMENTAL**CHANGES**

Strength and Power Exercises for Fighters

Over 30 Effective Exercises to Improve Strength & Power for Combat Athletes

ISBN: 978-1-78933-075-5

Published by **www.fundamental-lifestyle.com**

www.fundamental-lifestyle.com

Cover Image Copyright: Shutterstock:

For more information about the author:

Website: **www.5sfitness.co.uk**

Facebook: **www.facebook.com/5sfitnessuk**

Instagram: **www.instagram.com/5s_fitness**

Twitter: **www.twitter.com/5sfitness**

YouTube: **http://bit.ly/2GksRK1**

Other Books from Fundamental Lifestyle

Fix Your Posture:

The Simple Exercise Solution

Free Yourself from Aches and Pains Caused by Bad Posture

• Discover simple, yet life-changing posture correcting exercises and techniques.

• Understand how to fix your seated, standing and sleeping posture and reduce aches and pains.

• Build healthy posture habits that will have you living pain free.

20 Essential Exercises for Bigger Biceps: Quickly Build Big Biceps with Targeted Weightlifting Programs

Build big biceps in 20 easy exercises

• Learn how to build strength and muscle mass

• Develop healthy weight training habits

• Master workout programs to supercharge your gains

Strength and Mobility Exercises for Runners

Improve your Running Speed, Mobility and Strength

• Simple, effective exercises and example programs to follow

• Understand how to build strength, speed and mobility to become a better runner

• Build healthy training habits that will drastically improve and lengthen your running career

15 Essential Exercises for Bigger Triceps: Quickly Build Big Triceps with Targeted Weightlifting Programs

Discover simple yet effective exercises that build your triceps

• Safe training programs to reduce the risk of injury

• Diagrams and online videos to guide you

• Carefully planned program for maximum progress

The Gym Journal: A Workout Log Book The Ultimate Fitness Journal to Track Your Training and Achieve Your Exercise Goals

Includes professional advice from top UK coach on:

• Programming training for maximum benefit

• Effective warm-ups

• Strength and resistance training

This comprehensive training diary will help you track any kind of training.

The Daily Food Nutrition Journal: A Log Book & Food Diary to Track Your Eating Habits

Not just another log book / food diary...

• Accurately track and record your nutritional intake

• Discover your weaknesses: are you eating too much or too little?

• Monitor your long and short term goals

Contents

Introduction

Developing the correct techniques and appropriate skills for any sport should always come first, but today it is no longer good enough just to be highly skilled – strength plays a major role. All the elite men and women who compete at the top of their chosen sports are not only skilled technicians, but disciplined athletes. They put in the time and effort that helps them to compete at peak performance for longer and with greater consistency.

Similarly, when it comes to combat sports, you need to be in the best possible shape to compete, even at amateur level. Without developing the strength and conditioning to perform at your best, you will find your opponents quickly get the better of you – not because they are more skilled, but simply because they are stronger and have more stamina.

The goal of any good strength and conditioning coach, therefore, is to provide a training programme which complements the unique requirements of a particular sport – not just a person's ability to lift weights. If you take an educated approach to the development of your strength and power, working only 2-3 times per week, I guarantee you will reap the benefits.

This book teaches exercises specifically tailored for combat sports that will maximise your ability to produce strong, powerful strikes, and help you dominate your opponents in competition. Before getting stuck into the exercises, let's take a brief look at how to effectively develop both strength and power.

Anatomy of increasing performance - strength and power

Strength and power are the essential components in combat that govern your ability to strike an opponent. Understanding how to develop them is key to your progression as a fighter.

What is strength & power?

Strength is the ability to produce *force*. The more force you can produce to overcome a resistance, the stronger you are.

Explosive strength is the ability to produce maximal force in minimal time. An example of this is a fighter rapidly creating total body tension to hold their opponent down.

Power (which results from explosive strength), refers to *force* (strength) multiplied by *velocity* (speed), and is measured over a set distance. For example, power is needed to make an effective strike.

Strength (Force) x Speed (Velocity) = Power!

The terms *muscular endurance* and *strength endurance* are used to describe the ability of a competitor to express force many times over (i.e. making repeated hits and combos).

However, just because someone can produce a huge amount of force, it does not necessarily mean they can effectively use this force explosively.

This brings me to the paradox that exists between muscle force and velocity. Both force and velocity are required to produce power. Force can create faster movements, yet the corresponding muscle tension restricts speed. During a strike, therefore, it's not only essential for fighters to contract their muscles hard – they also need the ability to relax their muscles to create maximal speed.

In other words, during an outward strike, the initial movement contraction has to be followed by a relaxation phase, which is then quickly followed by a secondary contraction, just before the strike lands. The secondary contraction creates total body tension and puts the fighter's whole bodyweight behind the strike. This is referred to as the *double pulse*.

Striking performance is not just about how fast a muscle can produce force – it's also about how fast a muscle can relax to allow greater joint velocity.

Both the contraction and relaxation phases need to happen during every strike, and this is one of the reasons why big, strong people who haven't been trained to fight, can often throw a single hard punch, but look sluggish when attempting to perform numerous strikes against a moving opponent. They lack the motor skills to repeatedly execute the production of maximal force and joint velocity.

One aspect of strength that is often overlooked is that it ultimately dictates the robustness of your skeletal system and soft tissue. Without the ability to accommodate the loads or stresses placed on them, an athlete's development will be slowed or prevented by aches and injuries.

How do we develop strength and power?

Any form of movement/exercise will strengthen your structure to some extent, but our aim here is to optimise the benefits of training. If you have just 2 hours a week to dedicate to strength training for combat, what are the best exercises to perform, and how should we perform them?

When choosing exercises and deciding how to perform them, consider these three points.

The exercise should:

1. Maximise the weight that can be lifted i.e. maximise performance.

2. Maximise the work required by the muscles (*positive/adaptive stress*).

3. Minimise the *negative/maladaptive stress* placed on the supporting structures.

Building strength is a balance between these three points and the importance of each depends on your goals.

If you perform a full-depth squat (ass to grass), it will maximise muscular effort, but will also place more stress on the knees and reduce the amount of weight you can lift compared to a parallel squat.

On the other hand, a parallel squat allows you to lift heavier loads with less stress on the supporting structures. But your overall strength and muscular development won't be as good because the muscles aren't stressed through their full range of motion.

You need to find the optimal balance to achieve the best results for *your body* and your chosen sport, and this varies from person to person. Strengths and weaknesses differ, and so do the needs of different sports.

The most common method of strength development is to work at maximal or near maximal load for low rep ranges.

Dynamic effort

Less well known is the *dynamic effort* method. Dynamic effort lifting is simply lifting submaximal weights as fast as possible through the entire range of motion. This style of lifting helps you to get faster and stronger, as it teaches your nervous system/muscles to fire quickly. This generates more power than moving a weight slowly. However, caution must be taken as lifting weight at speed is stressful on your body.

It is important to lift heavy loads, as this will elicit the most strength gains, but you must also lift submaximal loads with maximum speed to develop your rate of force development.

It's clear that the ability to develop and unleash force quickly is essential for fighters: If you can produce force quickly, you will hit both harder and faster.

In this book I will introduce you to exercises that are optimal for strength and power development in fighters. I will teach you how to program these exercises and use *accommodating resistance* to maximise your benefits.

Accommodating resistance

In this section, I will teach you how to add accommodating resistance to various lifts. You can refer to this section when this technique is recommended in the exercises.

Accommodating resistance involves using bands and chains to *accommodate* resistance through the full range of motion of the lift. For example, placing heavy chains, or an anchored band over the ends of a barbell on a bench press means that the weight of the lift will increase as you raise the bar.

I suggest purchasing a set of four bands, which can be easily found on Amazon – red, black, purple and green.

During a lift such as a squat, deadlift or bench press, leverage is limited at the bottom of the movement and greatly increases as you progress through the lift. When a lift is performed without accommodating resistance, you must work hard initially to raise the bar. As your leverage improves, you don't need to produce as much force and must decelerate to control the bar at the top.

When accommodating resistance is added, the weight increases as you progress through the lift. So, as leverage improves, so does the load. Therefore, you must continually accelerate to complete the lift.

Accommodating resistance will train you to maximise your rate of force development.

When working with bands, more downward force is created by the bands in the eccentric (downward) phase, as they pull you down to the bottom of the movement. This is great for the development of power, but increased intensity will lead to increased fatigue and muscle soreness and therefore it shouldn't be overused.

If a lifter is *always* required to create maximal force through the range of motion, it doesn't allow them to naturally increase speed as leverage improves. This is an essential motor pattern to develop, because when you throw a punch you need to contract hard initially (create tension) before allowing speed and acceleration to increase through the movement to create power and a harder strike.

Don't train with accommodating resistance all the time, because it teaches you to keep a high level of tension through the lift and can cause excessive fatigue. For this reason, I recommend that you start by incorporating it into your dynamic effort sets. Once you have gained more experience, you can incorporate accommodating resistance into submaximal and maximal effort sets. Program it intelligently!

To perform any barbell exercise using a dynamic effort set, load 50-60% of your 1RM onto the barbell before attaching bands. We normally want the accommodating resistance to add 25% of your 1RM to the top of the lift. For example, if your 1RM is 100kg, then the accommodating resistance should add an extra 25kg at the top. This is easy to quantify with chains, but not so easy with bands.

The resistance (weight) added to the barbell by attaching bands can be hard to quantify because band tensions can vary due to the brand of band you are using, weathering, how they're attached, and many other factors. When using bands to create accommodating resistance during dynamic effort sets, I recommend attaching red bands and working from there. If you feel you can still lift fast with more band tension, then add more bands or use one with a higher tension. If start to lose speed throughout the lift, then reduce the tension. Experiment to find the optimal band tension for you.

To train speed and develop power without using accommodating resistance in dynamic sets, you can add 10-15% to the 50-60% of your 1RM to squats and deadlifts, and 5-10% of the 50-60% of your 1RM onto your presses. See what works for you – you just want to make sure the weight moves fast!

When adding accommodating resistance to heavy (90%+) sets, vary the band tension to optimise your results. This process is shown in the accompanying videos. Experiment by using both more weight from the plates with less band tension and vice versa.

Find what works for you and keep your training varied.

Breathing

The ability to regulate your breathing as a fighter is a very important tool. Firstly, it's important to breathe deeply through your belly using your diaphragm. This pulls your diaphragm down, expands your lungs, and consequently allows you to take in more oxygen.

The Diaphragm

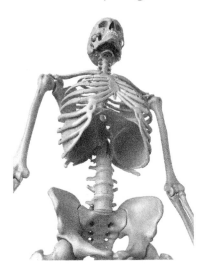

To practise diaphragmatic breathing, place one hand on your chest and one on your belly. Imagine a balloon low in your stomach. As you inhale through your nose or mouth the balloon expands, and as you exhale through your mouth it deflates. If your chest raises instead of your belly, your breathing is too shallow and you won't take in as much oxygen.

Many people breathe through the top of their chest, especially when mouth-breathing. This causes muscles that are not designed for respiration to overwork, and creates excess tension in unforeseen places, such as the neck muscles. Breathing at the top of the chest can also weaken the diaphragm through underuse and can result in fatigue during exercise and a performance reduction.

Nasal breathing increases rib cage and diaphragm engagement during inhalation. This is beneficial because it drives more oxygen into the lower lobes of your lungs compared to mouth breathing. However, nasal breathing may not allow you to draw in enough oxygen when working at a high intensity. Whether you use nasal or mouth breathing, the important thing is to maintain a constant rhythm, rather than randomly mixing the two.

While many experts agree that mouth breathing is the best way to take in oxygen at high intensities (some fighters may struggle breathing through their nose), if you can use nasal breathing while working at low to moderate intensities, I recommend you do so. Nasal breathing has also been shown to bring the heart and breath rate down more quickly during recovery.

Mouth breathing is often necessary for fighters to take in the oxygen they need. However, be careful not to overemphasise your breathing with a large open mouth as this will signal to you opponent that you are extremely fatigued. It can also increase the risk of jaw injuries.

Breathing while fighting

Regulating your breathing while fighting is incredibly important and can make the difference between a fighter feeling completely out of breath or completely in control.

Fighters should use an *anatomical* style of breathing where they synchronise their breath to match their movement. This style will involve slow and fast breathing.

Slow breathing is used when out of the opponent's range or between rounds. It involves breathing deeply and slowly to conserve energy, recover from previous attacks, strategize and calm the mind.

Fast breathing is used while attacking or being attacked by the opponent. It involves a slow or fast inhalation (depending on the situation) followed by short and quick exhalations (through the mouth) as the fighter performs strikes or quick defensive moves.

The exhalations are often quite loud and seem exaggerated but can really help to give the fighter a jolt of energy. The "psst" sound you often hear is not made by the fighter forcing all the air out quickly, but by them suddenly stopping the airflow to allow for numerous short, explosive exhalations as they strike.

Breathing during resistance training

During resistance training, we use a *biomechanical* style of breathing which maximises performance and minimises the risk of injury.

During biomechanical breathing, the athlete matches their inhalation with the downward (eccentric) phase of the exercise and their exhalation with the upward (concentric) phase. They normally exhale during the latter stage of the upward phase.

The Valsalva manoeuvre

Biomechanical breathing is normally coupled with the use of the Valsalva manoeuvre. This is "a moderately forceful attempted exhalation against a closed airway" (like equalizing your ears on an airplane by blowing against a pinched nose).

This manoeuvre, combined with a braced core, creates intra-abdominal pressure (IAP) and stabilises the spine. To visualise this, imagine the rigidity of a sealed plastic bottle full of air, compared to that of an open bottle.

Biomechanical breathing is an effective strategy. We can take this further by inhaling before starting the exercise and exhaling on completion. This, combined with the Valsalva manoeuvre, can cause a rise in blood pressure and dizziness. However, the performance benefits and reduced risk of injury generally outweigh the risks, barring other health considerations.

Compensatory acceleration

A key concept that helps to increase strength and power development is *compensatory acceleration.*

Compensatory acceleration to sports athletes is what mind-muscle connection is to bodybuilders. It is essentially making a conscious effort to maximise your force and speed throughout the entire range of motion. It is a great discipline to practice in its own right, but also very useful when you don't have the opportunity to apply accommodating resistance.

Often when you lift a heavy load, you grind out of the bottom (producing maximal force). However, as leverage improves, you make no effort to keep accelerating and often coast through the rest of the lift.

Mind muscle connection involves making a conscious effort to think about the muscle being worked. This helps to increase its engagement and ultimately stimulates greater muscular development. Both these methods will help you to maximise the effects of your training.

Common misconceptions

When it comes to physical development in any sport, strength plays a massive role and is often the primary target of strength and conditioning coaches. If an athlete is strong, sporting actions require less effort and the stresses caused by the activity are more easily handled.

Fighters have two common objections to strength training:

Won't strength training result in unnecessary bulk?

No.

The right kind of strength training will build lean muscle. For a fighter with a healthy diet and adequate training (pad work, sparring etc), two or three specifically designed strength sessions won't lead to excessive development of muscle mass. If it does, you should take up bodybuilding!

Won't strength training slow me down?

No.

If you concentrate *excessively* on the development of maximal strength by using heavy loads, then you may build muscle that is not necessarily fit for fighting. This could slow you down.

However, strength training will only negatively affect your performance when done to an *excessive* extent. A fighter should not prioritise lifting heavy weights. However, physiology clearly shows that some strength training is vital for the optimal performance of fighters.

Our muscles are made from both *fast twitch* and *slow twitch fibres*. These muscle fibres are used for different tasks. Slow twitch fibres are beneficial for marathon runners and fast twitch fibres are beneficial for sprinters.

As a fighter, you will benefit if you can effectively recruit both slow *and* fast twitch fibres. Not only do you require the muscular endurance to last the length of the whole fight, but you also need the explosiveness to up the intensity of your offensive work when necessary. Your fast twitch fibres are going to help you knock your opponent out!

To develop fast twitch fibres, you must incorporate high intensity strength training into your program.

Equipment

Here is a list of the equipment required to complete all the exercises in this book.

Any gym will have the basic bits of kit required to develop strength. The landmine attachment is the only bit of equipment that is a little more specialist and this exercise can be substituted with other *push* exercises.

Bands can easily be purchase on Amazon.

Equipment list:

- Barbell

- Hex/Trap Bar

- Plates – varying weights (ideally access to bumper plates)

- Dumbbells (dumbbells) – varying weights

- Kettlebells (KBs) – varying weights

- Weights Bench

- Landmine Attachment

- Ab Wheel

- Resistance Band – four colours (red, black, purple and green)

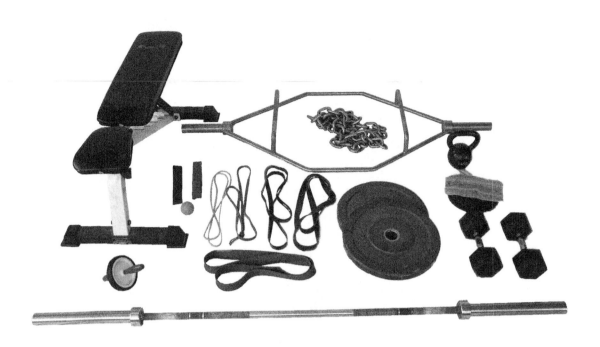

Get the Videos

The videos to accompany each exercise are available to download free from:

https://fundamental-changes.teachable.com/p/strength-exercises-for-fighters/

or here:

https://geni.us/fighters

Simply enrol in the course and you'll have **free access** to all the videos.

If you type the above link into a browser, please note there is no "www."

Chapter One: Shoulder Health

As a fighter, you will spend a lot of time in a guard stance that puts your shoulders into a hunched and rounded position. It is key that you strengthen the muscles that can become stressed through underuse, and mobilise the muscles that have become tense and restricted to keep your shoulders in good health and protect your posture.

Chest Release Technique & Stretch

The musculature of the chest is made up of the pectoralis major and the pectoralis minor (also known as the pecs). These muscles, specifically the pectoralis minor, can become tight due to prolonged rounded posture. This results in not only rounded shoulders, but tight chest muscles that constantly pull the shoulders into this position. If this is the case, the pectoral group needs to be released and stretched.

The Pectoralis Minor   The Pectoralis Major

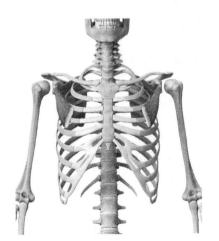
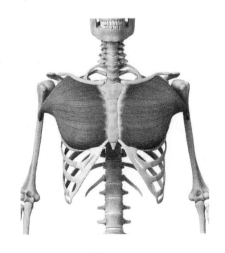

Massage Ball Release Technique:

Here's one of the easiest methods of releasing the pecs, specifically the pec minor.

1. Take a massage ball and place it against a wall/post at upper chest height.

2. Lean into the massage ball with your outer chest, just in from your armpit.

3. Hold your arm up to the side at shoulder height and horizontally flex and extend your arm forward and back (when working on a post or the corner of a wall) to increase the effects of the release technique.

4. Hold for 30-60 seconds.

5. Complete 1-2 times on each side.

Barbell Release Technique:

Here's an awesome release technique for the pec minor that can be performed with a barbell on the rack.

1. Set a barbell up on a rack at hip height.

2. Place your right arm over the barbell.

3. Drive the soft tissue between your chest and your arm into the barbell (just in from your armpit).

4. A weight (dumbbell/kettlebell) can be used to increase the pressure placed on the soft tissues.

5. Slowly move your arm forward and back and in small rotations (with or without weight).

6. Hold for 30-60 seconds.

7. Complete 1-2 times on each side.

Standing Chest Stretch:

This stretch can be performed in a doorway or the corner of a wall.

1. Raise your hand up with your elbow bent at 90 degrees.

2. Place your forearm along the edge of the door frame/wall and turn your body away from your arm.

3. Hold for 30-60 seconds for a regular stretch, or for 2 minutes if the musculature is very tense.

4. Complete 1-3 times.

Band External Rotations

If someone has a slouched upper body posture with rounded shoulders, their shoulders are often internally rotated. That is, their hands are rotated inwards so that their palms face behind them.

The rotator cuff is four deep muscles responsible for stabilising the shoulder joint, as well as its internal and external rotation. One muscle works as an internal rotator, while the other three work to externally rotate the shoulders. Pictured are two of the external rotators.

The internal rotator, along with your chest muscles, often gets plenty of work (due to repeated pushing/striking actions), whereas your external rotators are often underworked and can result in postural issues.

These postural issues cause all sorts of problems when you start to bench and overhead press at the gym. It is often said that "the bench press is bad for your shoulders", but actually it is poor posture and poor lifting mechanics that is bad for your shoulders.

It's vital that we develop muscles in a way that specifically target their different roles. The rotator cuff works to stabilise the shoulder joint as it performs various actions. Although creating external rotations may not be its main role, all muscles benefit from having their secondary and tertiary actions exercised and this exercise will create a deep burn in your shoulders!

Supraspinatus

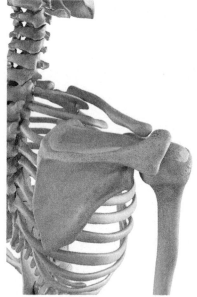

Infraspinatus

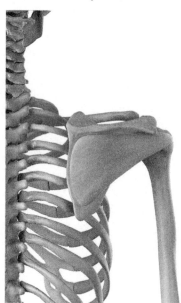

External Rotations – Long Band:

1. Attach a long band to something solid at abdominal height. Use a yellow or red band, increasing tension by standing further from the attachment point if required.

2. Grasp the band with your right hand and turn side-on, so that your left shoulder is closest to the attachment point.

3. Stand with good posture, bend your right elbow to 90 degrees and keep it tucked into your side.

4. Pull the band across your body while externally rotating your right shoulder. Ensure your body stays forward facing and your right elbow remains tucked into your side.

5. Once you have reached the limit of your range of motion with your elbow tucked in, slowly return to the starting position.

6. Don't allow the band to jerk you back to the starting position. Keep it controlled throughout the whole movement.

7. If your elbow comes away from your side, your large shoulder muscle (deltoid) will take over, so it's important to hold it close.

8. Complete 2-4 sets of 10 reps on each side.

External Rotations – Small Loop Band:

1. Small loop bands come in varying colours. For this exercise, you will need a low-tension band.

2. Hold the band with both hands. I usually place my thumbs over the band.

3. Bend your elbows at 90 degrees and keep both elbows tucked into your sides.

4. Externally rotate both shoulders at the same time.

5. Don't allow the band to jerk you back to the starting position. Keep it controlled through the whole movement.

6. Complete 2-4 sets of 10 reps

Band Pull Apart

I can't overstate how effective band pull apart variations are at restoring and maintaining shoulder health. Every client I have prescribed these to has had amazing results.

Band pull apart variations are especially good for fighters, but anyone who is looking to restore and maintain good upper-body posture and shoulder health will benefit from them.

During these exercises, it's important not to shrug your shoulders and bring your upper traps into play. You want to work the musculature of the upper back that is responsible for shoulder retraction, not elevation.

Standard Pull Apart:

1. Use a yellow or red long band. The tension can be varied by taking a wider or narrower grip.

2. Take an overhand grip (palms facing down) on the band and place your arms out in front of you with your elbows straight. Grip the band at shoulder width if you can.

3. With your arms straight, pull your arms outwards so the band stretches and comes to your mid chest.

4. The band can also be pulled to your abdomen or forehead to vary the angle at which your shoulders are working.

5. Don't allow the band to jerk you back to the starting position. Keep it under control through the whole movement.

6. Complete 2-4 sets of 10-20 reps.

Star Pattern:

The star pattern pull apart is a variation which cycles through various pulling positions.

1. Start with the standard pull apart to your mid chest.

2. Pull your right hand downwards and your left arm upwards so the band comes diagonally across your body.

3. Repeat this action but the opposite way around, right hand upwards and left hand downwards.

4. Repeat the standard pull apart to your upper chest to restart the cycle.

5. Complete 2-4 sets of 10-20 reps (each pull apart = 1 rep).

Banded Face-Pulls

Face-pulls are one of the best exercises to rehabilitate and develop your upper back and shoulders.

Resistance bands apply *accommodating resistance* to increase the engagement of your rear deltoids, traps and rhomboids as the band stretches during the face-pull.

1. Use a yellow or red band. You can alter the tension by standing closer or further away from the band attachment point.

2. Attach the band to something solid at chest height, either looping the band around and holding both ends, or looping the band through itself so you have hold of one end of the band with both hands.

3. Facing the attachment point, grab the band with an over-hand grip. Or, you can grasp the band with just your fingers, rather than a full grip, to help encourage the upper back to work as the primary mover rather than the biceps.

4. Step backwards to apply tension to the band.

5. Keep your chin back.

6. Pull backwards and slightly upward to bring yourself into a double bicep pose position. Maintain good head posture, pull your hands back to your temples and don't push your head towards the band.

7. Ensure you consciously engage your upper back and rear delts, rather than just pulling with your biceps. Visualise the muscle you are working to increase its engagement and build *mind-muscle connection*.

8. Return to the starting position under control, allowing your shoulders to extend slightly.

9. Complete 2-4 sets of 10-20 reps.

Band Front to Backs

The band front-to-back is an effective mobility drill for your shoulders that can be practised anytime. It mobilises all the muscles that restrict shoulder retraction and overhead positions, such as the pecs.

1. Grab a red band with a wide overhand grip. The wider your arms, the easier it is to take the band overhead and down towards your glutes.

2. The band gives you the freedom to widen your grip as you pass it overhead. Your grip should be wide enough so that you aren't forced to aggressively stretch the band out as you perform the movement, as this can cause you to shrug your shoulders, engaging musculature rather than promoting mobility.

3. Start with the band at your hips and while maintaining straight arms throughout, pass it overhead until it reaches your glutes, or the range of motion you can achieve.

4. Complete 2-4 sets of 5-10 reps.

Chapter Two: Squat

The squat is the foundation of your strength development and is the first of four primary strength movements (squat, push, hinge and pull).

As any good athlete knows, performance comes from the ground up and loaded squats will build a solid foundation in your legs. It's common to hear fighters complain about their legs tiring from simply moving around a ring or cage for three rounds.

There is a lot of debate regarding the correct depth for a squat. Some believe it necessary to go *ass to grass*. Others suggest a depth where their hamstrings are parallel to (or just below) the floor.

Joint anatomy and limb length play a key role in how people squat, but the depth I consider ideal involves squatting just below parallel, where the crease of your hips *just* passes the top of your knee caps. This maximises muscular engagement while maintaining the least stressful position on your knees and lumbar spine.

I will quickly describe the bodyweight squat before describing the three main squats in this chapter.

Bodyweight Squat:

1. Take a shoulder width stance with your toes pointing to the front or slightly outwards (no more than 30 degrees).

2. Initiate the movement with your hips, driving your glutes (buttocks) back.

3. As your hips hinge, bend your knees (almost simultaneously).

4. If your knees have a tendency to fall inwards (valgus), make a conscious effort to keep them in line with your toes by pushing them outwards.

5. As you squat, bring your hands to your front. This acts as a counter-balance as your centre of mass is tracking rearwards as you sit back into the squat.

6. Squat down to the appropriate depth (ideally breaking parallel).

7. At full depth, your knees will more than likely sit directly over your toes. Limb lengths can vary this. However, you don't want your knees to track too far forward of your toes as it places a lot of stress on them.

8. Drive back up out of the squat (the bottom is often referred to as *the hole*).

9. Complete 3-5 sets of 10-20 reps.

Goblet Squat

The goblet squat is an awesome variation that will help you to develop your squat mechanics.

This exercise was invented by strength coach Dan John and was named after the way the weight is held: high at the chest, as if holding a large goblet.

When novices perform bodyweight squats with little depth and excessive forward tilt of their torso, coaches often try to rectify any perceived mobility issues. However, *stability*, not mobility is often the underlying problem, as the person compensates for their centre of mass shifting rearwards.

A coach should give the novice a weight to hold, and the goblet position makes a perfect counterbalance to the weight of the body moving backward. The weight removes many of the stability issues and allows for greater depth to be achieved as their torso remains more upright. The goblet squat can literally progress someone with a terrible bodyweight squat, to squatting well within one set.

For a goblet squat, a kettlebell is usually used, but dumbbells or plates also work well.

1. Squat down and grab the horn (handle) of the kettlebell with both hands.

2. Lift the kettlebell and take a shoulder-width stance, with your toes pointing to the front or slightly outwards (no more than 30 degrees).

3. Initiate the movement with your hips, driving the glutes back.

4. As your hips hinge, bend your knees (almost simultaneously).

5. Lower under control, keep your knees in line with your toes.

6. Keep your elbows in, so that when you squat down, they comfortably fit in between your legs.

7. Once you have reached the appropriate depth, drive back up out of the squat.

8. Depending on the weight being used, complete 3-5 sets of 5-20 reps.

Back Squat

The back squat is considered by most to be the king of the squats, as it is the squat variant that allows you to load the most weight.

It is the first of three competitive powerlifts (back squat, bench press and deadlift). However, my aim here is to teach the foundations of strength development, not competitive lifting.

During the back squat, the barbell is held on your upper back. There are two distinct positions on the back that will affect the mechanics of the squat, but I won't get too hung up on which position to use, so find what works best for you.

High Bar Position: The barbell is held on the top of your upper traps, ensuring that it is *not* resting on the cervical vertebrae (distinct bony prominence on the back of the neck).

The barbell stays over your midfoot (halfway between your heel and toes, or the upper lacy part of the trainer) throughout the squat. If the barbell is high on your back, your torso requires less tilt to keep the barbell over the midfoot, so it stays more upright and allows for more depth.

During the high bar squat, leverage is weakest as you come to the parallel position (the point where your hips are most rearwards of the barbell). Making a conscious effort to drive your hips back under the barbell towards the end of the lift, brings you into a more mechanically efficient position. It maximises quad engagement and prevents your torso from falling forward.

Low Bar Position: The barbell is held 2-3 inches lower on your upper back, which will result in the barbell sitting behind your rear deltoids.

The reduced distance from your pelvis to the barbell can help to maximise the weight lifted. Therefore, competitive lifters often use a low bar position.

The low bar position does require a decent amount of shoulder mobility and can be quite uncomfortable if you are not used to it.

During a low bar squat, lifters will often use a *hip drive* method, where rather than driving your hips back under the barbell (which reduces the engagement of the hamstrings), you continue to drive upwards with your hips while maintaining a rigid back position (imagine driving upwards with your sacrum – upper buttocks).

Always do one or two warm-up sets with an unloaded barbell to get accustomed to the exercise. Find what style feels natural for you.

1. Set the barbell on the rack at upper chest height.

2. Grab the barbell 1-2 palms wider than shoulder-width with a comfortable grip (either full or false grip).

3. A full grip will often feel more stable for the lifter. However, a false grip (thumbs on same side as your fingers) allows your wrists to stay in a more neutral position (as your elbows are pointing rearwards). Take the grip which suits you.

4. Move your head under the barbell, placing the barbell into your preferred position on your traps – high or low bar position.

5. Walk under the barbell, so that your hips are directly underneath to ensure you don't lift the barbell off the rack with your lower back.

6. Lift the barbell up off the rack with your legs and take 2-3 short strides rearwards – a long walkout wastes energy and increases the risk of injury.

7. Adopt your squatting stance. Experiment with various stance widths and see what feels best for you (hip joint structure often dictates which stance width feels best for you).

8. Take a big gulp of air, brace your core (explained in Chapter 6: Core) and use the Valsalva manoeuvre (a moderately forceful attempted exhalation against a closed airway. Like equalizing your ears on an airplane by blowing against a pinched nose).

9. As you brace your core, pull down on the barbell to help increase total body tension.

10. Initiate the squat with your hips, driving your glutes rearwards, and bend your knees.

11. Allow your knees to track directly over your toes (this will vary depending on limb lengths).

12. Sit back to the point where you break parallel and your hip crease dips just below the top of your knee caps, or as deep as you can go while maintaining good form.

13. Use the stretch reflex (involuntary contraction in response to a stretch in the muscles) to recoil out of the hole.

14. Drive your shoulders into the barbell and your feet into the floor.

15. Pull down hard on the barbell as if you are trying to bend it over your back. This helps to maximise total body tension and muscular engagement.

16. Drive back up out of the squat.

17. Once you reach the top of the lift, exhale and get ready for the next rep.

18. When working with heavy loads, it's important that you treat every rep as a single, perfectly performed movement.

19. Depending on the weight being used, complete 3-5 sets of 2-10 reps.

Front Squat

The front squat is often considered the most "athletic" squat, partially due to its link to Olympic lifts which are the epitome of athletic prowess, but also because it builds many movements that are beneficial for athletic development.

During the front squat, the barbell is held to the front of the body in the front rack position, resulting in a more upright back angle compared to the back squat. This position helps to facilitate more depth, while also placing more load onto your quads (thighs).

Many people struggle to achieve the front rack position and, even if they can, often find it quite uncomfortable. This is due to the mobility required in the latissimus dorsi (lats – back muscles), triceps (muscles on the back of your arms) and forearms to hold the barbell comfortably on the anterior delts (front of your shoulders).

Mobility dictates to what extent the hands stay on the barbell. For a "clean and jerk" it is ideal to maintain as much grip as possible. However, during a front squat, it's not uncommon to see lifters have just their finger tips on the barbell.

Some people use a cross-armed position to hold the barbell, which is an easy alternative if the front rack position is inaccessible.

Although this position is fine to use, it is lacking in a few areas as it doesn't allow for the same level of thoracic tension and can result in a lack of symmetry between the shoulder blades.

The front rack position is optimal and should be practised if possible. Therefore, if you are unable to achieve it, I often regress the position using straps, as pictured below.

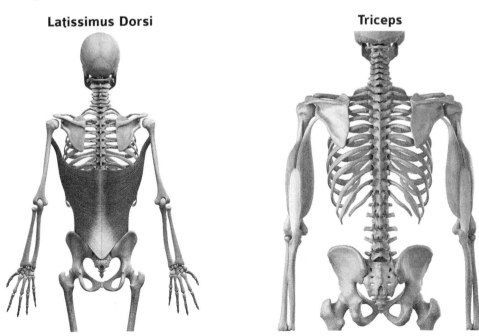

Latissimus Dorsi　　　　　　　　**Triceps**

1. Set the barbell on the rack at upper chest height.

2. Grab the barbell with your fingers slightly wider than shoulder width.

3. Take your elbows underneath the barbell so that the barbell sits in the crease that has been formed just

behind the bulk of your anterior delts. Your elbows will be facing forward (first picture).

4. Walk under the barbell so that your hips are directly underneath. This ensures you are not lifting the barbell off the rack with your lower back.

5. Lift the barbell up off the rack with your legs.

6. Take 2-3 short strides rearwards. Taking a long walkout wastes energy and increases the risk of injuries.

7. Adopt your squatting stance.

8. Take a big gulp of air, brace your core and use the Valsalva manoeuvre.

9. Initiate the squat by breaking at your hips, driving your glutes rearwards. However, the front squat will not use as much of a hinge as the back squat.

10. Bend your knees almost simultaneously.

11. Allow your knees to track to directly over your toes.

12. Squat to a point where you break parallel and your hip crease surpasses the top of your knee caps, or as deep as you can go while maintaining form. Full depth should be practised if you Olympic lift.

13. Use the stretch reflex to recoil out of the hole.

14. Drive your feet into the floor and lead with your chest and elbows to ensure your elbows stay high and you maintain the rigidity of your spine.

15. Once you reach the top of the lift, exhale and get ready for the next rep.

16. When working with heavy loads, it's important that you treat every rep as a single, perfectly performed movement.

17. Depending on the weight being used, complete 3-5 sets of 2-10 reps.

Chapter Three: Push

Push is the second of the four primary strength movements and is vital in the development of the upper body striking muscles – pectorals (chest), anterior deltoids (front of shoulder), triceps and the serratus anterior (pictured).

There are two main variations of the push movement: horizontal and vertical. Both will be introduced in this chapter.

I will also introduce variations that are specifically designed to transfer force from your lower body to your upper body. This happens in an effective muscle chain during a punch. A foot pivots, a hip extends, and power is transferred from your legs, through your torso and into your fist.

The Serratus Anterior
Used in far reaching movements – a strike

Bench Press

The bench press is by far the most used barbell exercise in a commercial gym environment with "What can you bench?" seeming to be the only judge of strength.

The bench has gained a reputation for being *unfunctional*, as you are lying on a bench. However, it is one of the most effective ways of developing your pushing muscles. Therefore, it is incredibly *functional*.

The bench press is a horizontal pushing exercise which involves pressing a barbell while lying on a bench. It will build strength in your chest, shoulders, triceps and lats – all of which are important for striking.

A great variation of the bench press is the close grip bench press (pictured below) which places more emphasis on the triceps. This involves taking a much narrower grip, but not to the extent where it negatively affects the wrists (a common mistake). It is a great variation for fighters as it uses an elbow position more specific to punching.

1. Lie on the bench so that your eyes are directly under the barbell.

2. Grab the barbell 1-2 palm's distance wider than shoulder width apart. An ideal grip placement leaves your forearms perpendicular to the barbell at the bottom of the lift.

3. Some lifters use a false grip. However, I recommend taking a full grip on the barbell and squeezing it as tight as possible (squeezing the barbell tightly will increase rotator cuff engagement).

4. Pull your heels rearwards, push your knees back and drive your soles into the floor. Some lifters come up onto their toes and that's fine – find what works for you.

5. Pull your shoulder blades inwards and down and drive your upper back into the bench. This will facilitate a slight arch in your lower back, leaving two points of contact on the bench (glutes and upper back).

6. Don't worry about having a slight arch in your lower back while holding the barbell. The load is perpendicular to your spine and so is not compressing it as it would during a back squat.

7. If you suffer with low back pain, exaggerating the arch can sometimes be stressful (back pain exacerbated by extension). If this is the case, simply reduce the extent at which you are arching or take it away completely (this is one of the reasons you see people with their knees up – it flattens the lower back).

8. Pull the barbell off the J-cups ensuring you do not unset your position. If the J-cups are set too low or too high, it often causes you to unset your shoulder blades.

9. Hold the barbell at the top and take a big gulp of air, brace your core and use the Valsalva manoeuvre.

10. Lower the barbell under control until it comes to your lower chest.

11. Use the stretch reflex without bouncing the barbell off your ribcage.

12. Press the barbell up while driving your upper back into the bench.

13. Once you reach the top of the lift, exhale and get ready for the next rep.

14. When working with heavy loads, it's important that you treat every rep as a single, perfectly performed movement.

15. Depending on the weight being used, complete 3-5 sets of 2-10 reps.

Floor Press

The floor press is a horizontal barbell press performed on the floor. Performing a press from this position has numerous benefits.

The floor press reduces the range of motion (ROM) as the back of your arms hit the floor. It therefore places more emphasis on your anterior delts and triceps, rather than your chest and lats. This ROM allows you to lift heavy loads while reducing the stress placed on your shoulder joints.

Lying on the floor with your legs straight also takes away any leg drive, which creates a true upper body push.

1. Set the barbell up on a rack at a height that leaves it in the same position it would be in if you were lying on a bench (the floor being the bench).

2. Grab the barbell 1-2 palms distance wider than shoulder width apart. An ideal grip placement leaves your forearms perpendicular to the barbell at the bottom of the lift.

3. Some lifters use a false grip. However, I recommend taking a full grip on the barbell and squeezing it as tight as possible (squeezing the barbell tightly will increase rotator cuff engagement).

4. Keep your legs straight.

5. Pull your shoulder blades inwards and down and drive your upper back into the floor.

6. Pull the barbell off the J-cups ensuring you do not unset your position. If the J-cups are set too low or too high, it often causes you to unset your shoulder blades.

7. Hold the barbell at the top and take a big gulp of air, brace your core and use the Valsalva manoeuvre.

8. Lower the barbell under control (towards your lower chest) until the back of your arms touch the floor.

9. Press the barbell up while driving your upper back into the floor.

10. Once you reach the top of the lift, exhale and get ready for the next rep.

11. When working with heavy loads, it's important that you treat every rep as a single, perfectly performed movement.

12. Depending on the weight being used, complete 3-5 sets of 2-10 reps.

Overhead Press

The overhead press is by far the most underused barbell exercise.

This is partly because it's not one of the three powerlifts (squat, bench, deadlift), and is not used in its strict form in Olympic lifting.

It is also one of the hardest exercises to facilitate with any reasonable weight compared to the other primary lifts, hence some people shy away from it.

It takes an unbelievable amount of strength and stability to stand like a pillar and press a heavy weight overhead. Not only that, it requires good mobility and lifting mechanics to maintain a press that isn't placing huge amounts of stress on the supporting structures, such as your lower back.

There are a few variations of this movement, each done with varying degrees of *strictness*.

The terms *strict press* or *military press* describe a pressing action that doesn't use the lower body in any way. It only uses upper body movement, with no prior action to help generate upward drive i.e. a knee bend.

The next exercise on the list is the push press, which is like the strict press, but uses a knee drive, meaning the barbell is propelled upwards using the lower body.

1. Set the barbell on the rack at upper chest height.

2. Grab the barbell slightly wider than shoulder width apart. A false grip can be beneficial as it allows you to set the barbell up on the base of your palms, which aligns your forearms directly under the barbell. However, a full grip increases the engagement of your rotator cuff – find which one works best for you.

3. Bring your elbows forward so they sit directly under the barbell. While in this position, the barbell should rest on your upper chest. However, if your forearms are long in relation to your upper arms, then the barbell may not sit on your chest. This is not an issue, it just means you may have to hold all the load with your arms.

4. Stand underneath the barbell and use your legs to lift it off the rack. Take 2-3 short strides rearwards and adopt a hip-shoulder width stance.

5. Squeeze your glutes, engage your core and drive your chest upwards and your head back out of the way of the barbell.

6. Take a big gulp of air and utilise the Valsalva manoeuvre.

7. Press the barbell upwards without any leg drive (bending and straightening your knees).

8. Once the barbell passes your head, shrug your upper back. This will bring your torso and head underneath the barbell.

9. The barbell should travel upward in a vertical path. However, because of the shrugging action (which brings your torso underneath the barbell) the barbell will start over your upper chest and finish over the back of your neck.

10. Once you reach the top of the lift, lower the barbell back to your upper chest, exhale and get ready for the next rep.

11. When working with heavy loads, treat every rep as a single, perfectly performed exercise.

12. Depending on the weight being used, complete 3-5 sets of 2-10 reps.

Push Press

The push press is an overhead press variation. In this case, a leg drive (knee bend) is used to propel the barbell up off your shoulders, so there are a few setup differences.

The push press can be performed with the same setup as the strict press. However, it is beneficial to work from the front rack position to better facilitate the initial leg drive. This is because the strict press setup creates too much tension in the arms and therefore limits your ability to transfer force from your lower body into the barbell.

Pressing actions which use leg drive are a fantastic way to develop total body strength and power, producing force from your lower body and expressing it through your upper body.

1. Set the barbell on the rack at upper chest height.

2. Set yourself up in a front rack position (the setup used for the overhead press can be used if you are unable to effectively use the front rack technique).

3. Take a big gulp of air, brace your core and use the Valsalva manoeuvre.

4. Bend your knees and sit back with your hips slightly.

5. Accelerate up and propel the barbell up off your shoulders.

6. As the barbell is propelled upwards, punch your arms underneath to extend the barbell overhead.

7. Due to the explosiveness of the movement, it is fine to exhale at the top of the lift. However, it is always beneficial to maintain intraabdominal pressure until the entire rep is completed.

8. Once the barbell is at the top, lower it down under control and catch it on your anterior delts with a slight dip of your knees to absorb the impact.

9. When working with heavy loads, it's important that you treat every rep as a single, perfectly performed movement.

10. Depending on the weight being used, complete 3-5 sets of 2-5 reps.

Landmine Single Arm Press / Strike & Split Jerk

The landmine is an invaluable piece of equipment that has become synonymous with the development of fighters because many landmine drills are similar to throwing upper body strikes.

In this section, I will describe the basics of pressing the landmine and one of my favourite landmine drills: the landmine split jerk.

Landmine Single Arm Press / Strike:

1. Grab the barbell in your right hand and hold it at your right shoulder.

2. Place your left foot in front of your right.

3. You can place the same foot forward as the hand you are pressing/striking with. This mimic's the positioning of a jab. However, you will produce more force with your right foot to the rear while pressing/striking with the right hand.

4. Press the barbell until your elbow is fully extended. This can be performed explosively in the form of a strike.

5. Exhale at the top of the movement.

6. Inhale as you bring the barbell back to your shoulder, or take a deep breath while the barbell is at your shoulder before continuing with successive reps.

7. Repeat on each side.

8. Depending on the weight being used, complete 3-5 sets of 5-10 reps.

Landmine Split Jerk:

1. Grab the barbell in your right hand and hold it at your right shoulder.

2. Stand with a hip-shoulder width stance.

3. Dip down with your knees as if you are performing a push press. Create total body tension before releasing tension (relaxation phase) to allow the barbell to accelerate as you throw the barbell forward.

4. Propel the barbell off your shoulder and as you do so, split your stance so that your left leg is to the front (opposite to the hand performing the press).

5. As your feet land, your arm should be fully extended, and both your feet should be slightly internally rotated (toes inwards slightly) to maximise stability.

6. Exhale at the top of the movement and engage total body tension (double pulse).

7. Bring the barbell back to your shoulder, reset your stance and get ready for successive reps.

8. See every rep as an single, perfectly performed rep.

9. Repeat on each side.

10. Depending on the weight being used, complete 3-5 sets of 2-5 reps on each side.

Dumbbell Clean & Press

Dumbbell variations of the clean and press and snatch (covered in the next chapter), are easy to master compared to their barbell counterparts.

Although they are relatively simple exercises, they are great for building explosive strength and overall conditioning.

This dumbbell clean and press variation involves firing the dumbbells up from a hang (lower/mid-thigh) position and catching them in a power clean position (above parallel squat). Before push pressing or push jerking them overhead.

A *jerk* involves a secondary knee bend after the initial knee drive to propel the weight overhead. This second knee bend locks your arms out.

1. Hold the dumbbells at your side.

2. Hinge your hips and bend your knees to bring the dumbbells down to your lower/mid-thigh.

3. Explosively triple extend (extension of ankles, knees and hips), shrug your shoulders and pull your elbows upwards and rearwards.

4. As the dumbbells elevate, dip down into a quarter squat and catch the dumbbells in a rack position (at your shoulders).

5. Recover from this quarter squat position before re-dipping with your knees and propelling the dumbbells off your shoulders.

6. If using a jerk, re-dip with your knees to extend your elbows.

7. Bring the dumbbells back to your shoulders, absorbing any impact with a slight dip of your knees.

8. Bring the dumbbells back to your sides, ensuring you don't swing them rearwards, but instead drop them down to the lower/mid-thigh position before continuing successive reps.

9. If done with heavier loads, see every rep as a single, perfectly performed rep.

10. Depending on the weight being used, complete 3-5 sets of 5-20 reps.

Chapter Four: Hinge & Pull

Hinge and pull are the third and fourth primary strength movements, although the hip hinge is the first movement I teach my clients, as it is integral to human function and vital in the development of strong, powerful hips.

The hip hinge involves you bending at your hips to allow your torso to drop forward while maintaining a neutral (unbent and untwisted) spine. It is an essential movement pattern that allows you to perform daily tasks like picking an object up off the ground without compromising your back.

Hinge exercises are the most effective to develop your posterior chain, specifically the hamstrings and glutes, which are your "engine" when producing strength and power.

The Gluteus Maximus

The Biceps Femoris – one of the Hamstrings

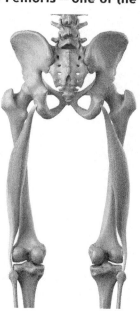

Hinge movements are often combined with, or even described as, pulling actions, as they are both working the muscles on the posterior side of the body (i.e. pulling the barbell off the floor or rowing a barbell in a hinged position).

Upper body pulling movements, which work the musculature of the mid-upper back and the biceps are also vitally important to daily function and sports performance. These muscle groups help you to deliver strong and stable strikes and help you to hold your opponent in place if needed.

Training the mid-upper back will also help to keep your shoulders and upper spine in good health.

Deep Back Muscles   **Superficial Back Muscles**

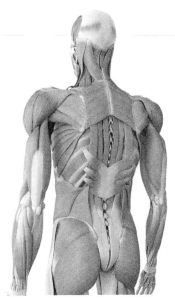 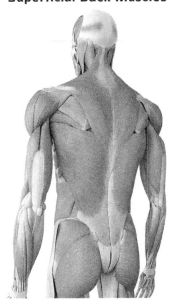

Here's how to correctly perform a bodyweight hip hinge.

1. Stand with soft knees and good upper body posture, ensuring your chest is proud and remains so throughout the movement.

2. Initiate the movement by driving your glutes rearwards. Standing a trainer's distance from a wall and attempting to touch the wall with your glutes works as a great teaching aid.

3. Maintain the soft knee position and keep driving your glutes rearwards, this will cause your hips to hinge, dropping your torso forward.

4. Keep going until you feel your hamstrings reach the extent of their ROM. Ensure you maintain a neutral spine.

5. With straight legs (soft knees) and a neutral spine, this will usually bring your torso to parallel or just above parallel to the floor.

45

Rack Pull

The rack pull involves pulling a barbell up to your hips from a set height on a rack or set of blocks.

The height is usually set so the barbell starts just below your knee caps. However, any height can be used to work various ranges of the pull.

Transitioning across your knee caps is the section of the lift where most load is placed on your lower back as this is the point where your pelvis is furthest from the barbell.

If you start with the barbell above your knees, more emphasis is placed on your glutes locking out your hips. I suggest also working from this position.

The rack pull is a great exercise to learn the mechanics of the hinge. It acts an ideal progression towards the deadlift, and due to the reduced ROM, and in turn good leverage, you can increase the loads, intensifying the work on your glutes and back.

1. Set the pins/spotter bars on a rack at just below knee height (blocks can be used).

2. Place the barbell on the pins and stand with your midfoot directly under the barbell, leaving your legs about an inch away.

3. Hip hinge and bend your knees slightly so that you can grab the barbell with an overhand or alternated grip (one hand overhand, one hand underhand).

4. Sit back with your glutes and drive your chest up. This will bring your legs forward into the barbell.

5. Take a big gulp of air, brace your core and use the Valsalva manoeuvre. As you do this, take the slack out of the barbell (slack between the barbell and plates) by pulling on it slightly. This also helps to create total body tension.

6. Drive your heels into the floor, maximally engage your glutes and back and pull the barbell upwards and rearwards off the rack. Ensure you allow time for inertia to be broken.

7. Squeeze your glutes and upper back hard at the top.

8. Lower the barbell back down to the pins under control, exhale and get ready for the next rep.

9. When working with heavy loads, it's important that you treat every rep as a single, perfectly performed movement.

10. Depending on the weight being used, complete 3-5 sets of 2-10 reps.

RDL - Romanian Deadlift

The RDL is my lift of choice when progressing fighters from a bodyweight hinge to working with weight. It acts as a great prerequisite to the deadlift.

It is also one of the best exercises for developing your posterior chain and, in turn, developing strong, powerful hips.

1. Start with the barbell at your hips with a pronated (overhand) grip. Ensure you pick the barbell up with good form, while maintaining a neutral spine.

2. Initiate the movement by driving your glutes back and bending your knees slightly. Allow your shoulders to come over the barbell while it maintains contact with your legs.

3. Keep driving your glutes back to facilitate the hinge and allow the barbell to track down your quads. If there is too much knee bend at this point, the barbell will sit on your quads, rather than track down smoothly.

4. Once the barbell passes your knee caps, bend your knees slightly to bring the barbell to about a palm's distance below your knees.

5. Engage the glutes and bring the barbell back up your legs, following the same path it went down. Maintain a vertical bar path throughout (if someone were watching from the side, they would see the barbell move in a vertical line).

6. Squeeze your glutes hard at the top to get them firing and proceed with successive reps.

7. When working with heavy loads, it's important that you treat every rep as a single, perfectly performed movement.

8. Depending on the weight being used, complete 3-5 sets of 5-8 reps.

Deadlift

The deadlift is the king of the hinge and pull movements, and is fundamental to the development of strong, powerful hips.

Please note that lifting a heavy weight off the floor can stress your spine in a way that can cause injury. It is essential that you perform this exercise with good form.

It should be noted, however, that injuries are not just a matter of technique or poor form. Regardless of whether you lift correctly or not, if your soft tissues haven't got the strength to handle the load (even with perfect form), injuries such as straining your lower back muscles can occur.

When it comes to the deadlift, many people are hell-bent on going as heavy as they can on every session, even if it's the first time they have lifted a barbell off the floor. However, to make real physical progression, you need to develop every link within the kinetic chain that is your body and *progressive programming* (gradually becoming harder) will allow all your structures to adapt, remembering that some structures (particularly smaller muscles involved in joint stabilisation) may not develop as quickly as others.

The lower back is one of the most important links within the kinetic chain. Without strength in this area we not only compromise performance, but also risk serious, life-changing injury.

Do not underestimate the importance of the lower back – it truly is an integral part of your ability to maintain posture and maximise performance.

The Quadratus Lumborum

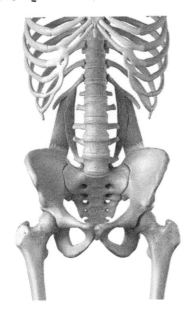

The Erector Spinae

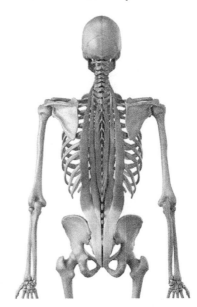

1. Set the barbell up on the floor with 45cm plates.

2. Approach the barbell so that your midfoot is directly underneath it. Your shins should be an inch away from the barbell.

3. Hinge with your hips and bend your knees until you can grab the barbell.

4. Take a pronated or alternated grip. Use a pronated grip as much as possible to develop your grip strength.

5. Sit back with your glutes and drive your chest up. This will bring your shins forward until they come into contact or are just off the barbell.

6. Take a big gulp of air, brace your core and use the Valsalva manoeuvre. As you do this, pull on the barbell slightly to create total body tension and take the slack out of the barbell and plates.

7. Drive your heels into the floor and pull the barbell upwards and rearwards off the floor. Allow time for the inertia of the barbell to be broken. You must produce enough force to break the weight off the floor, and this doesn't always happen as soon as you start pulling.

8. Engage your lats (back) to keep the barbell within its vertical path.

9. Once the barbell passes your knees, drive your hips into it and push your chest up. Your shoulders will fall naturally behind the barbell. There is no need to shrug or throw your shoulders rearwards.

10. Once you have finished locking out your hips, drive your glutes rearwards and bend your knees slightly to allow the barbell to track down your legs smoothly (just like the RDL).

11. Once the barbell passes your knee caps, bend your knees until the plates touch the floor.

12. At the bottom, exhale and get ready for the next rep.

1. Don't bounce the plates off the floor to create upward momentum. When working with heavy loads, it's important that you treat every rep as a single, perfectly performed movement.

13. Depending on the weight being used, complete 3-5 sets of 2-5 reps.

Hex Bar Deadlift

The hex bar (often referred to as the trap bar) deadlift, is one of the best deadlift variations and is considered by many to be superior to the conventional deadlift for athletic development. Studies have shown that lifters can often lift heavier, with greater speed and power, while deadlifting the hex bar.

Another benefit of the hex bar deadlift is the ease of the setup. Often people struggle to perfect their conventional deadlift positioning. However, due to the nature of the hex bar setup, with the hands placed to the sides rather than at the front, the position often comes naturally.

Bearing in mind all this information you may question, why not just use the hex bar deadlift?

The hex bar does have huge benefits. However, it is an exercise in itself. The setup turns the exercise into more of a squatting movement with greater load placed on your quads. (Some even refer to the movement as a hex bar squat).

The conventional deadlift on the other hand, places more load on your posterior chain, which as discussed previously, is vital for overall strength development and athletic performance. I suggest using both variants, not only for increased performance and a reduced risk of injury, but because it will help to mix up your training and keep things interesting.

1. Stand within the hex bar, with 45cm plates loaded onto it.

2. Squat down with an exaggerated hip hinge and grasp the bars on either side.

3. Sit back to load your quads and drive your chest up.

4. Take a big gulp of air, brace your core and use the Valsalva manoeuvre. As you do this, pull on the hex bar slightly to create total body tension and take the slack out of the hex bar and plates.

5. Drive your feet into the floor and raise the hex bar up until your legs are fully extended.

6. Return the hex bar to the floor.

7. At the bottom, exhale and get ready for the next rep.

2. Don't bounce the plates off the floor. When working with heavy loads, it's important that you treat every rep as a single, perfectly performed movement.

8. Depending on the weight being used, complete 3-5 sets of 2-10 reps.

Hex Bar Jumps

Hex bar jumps are one of my favourite loaded jump exercises.

Jumping actions, Olympic lifts and many of their variations are synonymous with athletic development as they involve *triple extension* – explosively taking your ankles, knees and hips from a flexed position to an extended position.

If you break down sporting actions, you will see that the triple extension is the driving force of many movements, not only running and jumping. It is used each time you throw a strike.

Loaded jumps with the barbell/hex bar are among the most underused tools and can be used to significant effect.

Loaded jumps can be performed with a barbell on your back (usually performed at 30-40% of 1RM). However, jumping is inherently stressful on your joints, even without added weight. Therefore, it is essential that the correct progressions are made so that you can handle the stress.

Hex bar jumps are one of the most effective ways to perform loaded jumps. Not only is the set up easy, with heavy loads easily applied, but the nature of the loading position allows you to de-load much of the weight as it travels back towards the floor. Although you don't release control of the hex bar entirely, you can release tension through the downward phase.

1. Set up as you would for the hex bar deadlift.

2. Take a big gulp of air, brace your core and use the Valsalva manoeuvre. As you do this, take the slack out of the hex bar.

3. Drive upwards as you would during the deadlift. However, carry on accelerating at the top to turn it into a jump (triple extension).

4. On landing, keep control of the hex bar and progress straight into the downward phase. Your grip can be released slightly (letting the hex bar fall under control), reducing the impact greatly.

5. Ensure you maintain enough control of the hex bar so you can effectively perform successive reps.

6. Depending on the weight being used, complete 3-10 sets of 2-10 reps.

Power Clean

Olympic lifts are often seen as the pinnacle of athletic prowess as they involve explosive triple extension, while requiring you to control the barbell and quickly receive it in a position that demands huge amounts of stability and mobility.

The power clean starts just like the full clean. Rather than receiving it in a full squat, however, you catch the barbell in a higher position. For a lift to be classed as a power clean, you must stop above a parallel squat position or higher and stand up from there.

The power clean also forces a lifter to perform a violent second pull (explained in the exercise description) and a fast turn-over (third pull) of the barbell to receive it in the higher position. Essentially, the power clean promotes the need for speed and aggression.

For Olympic lifts, the *hook grip* is the grip of choice. This is where your thumb is trapped between the barbell and your first and second finger. Make sure your thumb is wrapped around the barbell and not just pinned parallel to the bar.

The hook grip is an extremely strong pronated grip that allows the lifter to hold the barbell without having to apply too much grip tension. This reduces elbow tension during the lifts and allows for better power transfer from the legs to the barbell. It also allows for a more fluid transition into catching the barbell in the front rack position.

The hook grip can be used on other barbell lifts such as the deadlift. Its only downfall is that it can be quite uncomfortable, with the main solution to the discomfort being, "Dry your eyes and get used to it"!

This is a complicated lift, so it is essential to view the video before attempting this, and I highly recommend working with a professional coach to develop your skills.

1. The first pull is a *clean* deadlift (off the floor to above your knees), with a hip-width stance and a slightly wider than shoulder width grip placement. The grip placement needs to allow you to receive the barbell in the front rack position. Find what suits you.

2. The clean deadlift involves you sitting back a little more than you might during a conventional deadlift (you will feel the load on your quads). Ensure you drive your chest up and retract your shoulder blades to tighten up your back. Your shoulders will be over the barbell.

3. Rotate your elbows out to the sides in line with the barbell. Keep your arms straight and look straight ahead.

4. The first pull involves pulling the barbell up to just past your knees (it starts slowly and accelerates as you transition into the second pull). Imagine driving the weight up with your quads (drive your feet into the floor), maintaining a rigid spine as your shoulders come slightly in front of the barbell. Keep the barbell close, but don't drag it up your shins (maintain a vertical bar path).

5. Now the barbell is past your knees, you are transitioning into the second pull. This is where you accelerate the barbell up your quads (don't cause too much friction by excessively dragging it up your legs).

6. Explosively drive your hips/pelvis into the barbell and triple extend (jump with the barbell). The barbell needs to travel up high towards the top of your quads. A common fault is firing the barbell off your legs too early. The position where the barbell fires off the hips (top of quads) is referred to as the *power position*.

7. As the barbell travels up past your hips, shrug the barbell up with your traps/shoulders and pull your elbows upwards and rearwards, keeping the barbell as close to your body as possible.

8. Once you are in full triple extension and have maximised the second pull, consciously pull yourself under the barbell (third pull). Shooting down into the power clean receiving position (parallel squat or higher).

9. As you pull yourself under the barbell, rotate your elbows underneath the barbell to catch it in the front rack position.

10. As you drop down into the receiving position, your feet will spread slightly to facilitate a more comfortable squatting stance.

11. The stance only needs to be slightly wider than your starting stance. It's common to hear some lifters weightlifting shoes slam down as they receive the barbell, but ensure you don't hinder the movement by exaggerating this with too much of a stomp. The transition of the feet needs to be quick and efficient.

12. Once you have received the barbell, recover to a standing position.

13. When working with moderate loads you can take the barbell back down to the floor under control. However, you can drop the barbell from the front rack position. When Olympic lifting, it usually makes more sense to drop the barbell as it reduces the risk of injury and limits excessive fatigue.

14. Complete 5-8 sets of 1-3 reps.

KB Swing

The kettlebell swing is a *ballistic* hip hinge movement that develops explosive hip extension and, in turn, explosive strikes. Ballistic movements involve maximum acceleration and velocity over short periods of time. It is essential that both the upward and downward phases of this lift are completed with good speed.

Ballistic movements are commonly associated with injuries, because it's harder to maintain control over fast movements and they place more stress on the soft tissues. However, the actions we perform in sports like boxing and MMA, are generally ballistic in nature, so it's important to incorporate ballistic actions into your training.

There are two main styles of swing: the Russian swing, which brings the kettlebell to chest height, and the American swing, which brings the kettlebell overhead.

We will be looking at the Russian swing.

The true purpose of the kettlebell swing is to facilitate a ballistic extension of the hips. Once the kettlebell reaches chest height, you have achieved full extension and any further movement overhead simply detracts from this. If the kettlebell easily surpasses chest height, use a heavier weight to maximise muscle recruitment.

At the bottom of the lift (where the kettlebell is between your legs), your knees should be slightly bent. The kettlebell swing does not involve a squatting action.

It works well to exhale at the bottom of the movement, while your ribcage and stomach are compressed, and inhale at the top of the movement, while your rib cage is expanded.

1. Place the kettlebell an arm's length in front of you.

2. Take a shoulder-width or slightly wider stance with soft knees. Hinge at the hips and drive your glutes rearwards. This will bring your torso just above parallel to the floor.

3. Grab the horn (handle) of the kettlebell.

4. Explosively pull the kettlebell rearwards into the *back swing* (the position where the kettlebell is between/behind your legs). Your arms should be high in your groin. If they are not, stress is placed on your lower back, rather than spread through your glutes and hamstrings.

5. Once the kettlebell has reached the end of the back swing, explosively contract your glutes and hamstrings to fire the kettlebell up to chest height.

6. From chest height, allow the kettlebell to swing back down in a fast, but controlled manner. Perform a full back swing (keeping your arms high in your groin) and continue with successive reps.

7. Depending on the weight being used, complete 3-5 sets of 5-20 reps.

Single Arm Rows

Single arm rows are great for both single arm pulling strength and overall shoulder and upper back health.

The single arm row also acts as a great anti-rotation and anti-flexion exercise, and the variation that I will be teaching maximises this and requires plenty of engagement from your lower body to support the movement.

Performing this lift with one knee on the bench is an effective way to perform rows. However, I prefer to support with one hand as I feel it maximises the need for a solid base and setup.

There are many row variations which are set up with varying shoulder heights in relation to your hips. The higher your shoulders, the more the lift will work your upper back. A more parallel position will engage more mid-upper back.

Here I will be teaching a position set just above parallel with your shoulders slightly higher than your hips.

1. Single arm rows can be done with the knee and hand on the same side supported on a bench, or with just one hand on a bench as support. I personally prefer a single hand support.

2. For the single hand supported row, hinge at your hips and bend your knees slightly, placing your right hand on the bench.

3. Your feet should be slightly wider than shoulder width apart, either side by side or in a *split stance* where the same leg of the arm rowing is behind you.

4. Rows can be done with your torso parallel to the floor. However, a position where your shoulders are slightly higher than your hips will work the upper back more.

5. Bend your knees to pick up the dumbbell before raising it up 5-10 inches off the floor.

6. Pull the dumbbell up to your side, ensuring you consciously engage your back and posterior (rear) delts to retract your shoulders.

7. Lower the dumbbell, keeping it under control, and allow your shoulders to protract slightly to stretch the muscles of your back.

8. Complete 3-5 sets of 8-20 reps on each side.

Dumbbell Snatch

Just like the dumbbell clean and press, the dumbbell snatch is a brilliant total body exercise that is easy to master and makes a great conditioning exercise.

This exercise forces you to perform a powerful pull and extension of your hips, and due to it being unilateral (working one side at a time), works rotational strength.

The need to decelerate and control the dumbbell at the top develops shoulder stability.

1. Stand with a shoulder width or slightly wider stance.

2. Squat down with a prominent hip hinge and grab the dumbbell which is placed between your legs in line with your midfoot-toes.

3. Don't place your none-lifting hand on your leg, have it off to the side or behind your back.

4. Drive your feet into the floor and explosively pull the dumbbell up, keeping it close to your body in a vertical path. It is important to allow your posterior chain and quads to do the work, rather than seeing your arm as the driving force.

5. As you triple extend (jump), pull your elbow upwards and rearwards, again keeping the dumbbell close to your body.

6. As you reach the top of the pull, punch your fist through and dip underneath to receive the dumbbell in a power snatch position (quarter squat), before recovering and standing up straight.

7. When working with moderate loads, bring the dumbbell back down to the floor under control by kinking your wrist and allowing the dumbbell to follow the same vertical path that it took on the way up. Starting at this point is an effective way to instil the concept of a vertical path close to your body.

8. When working with heavier loads, it can be safer to bring the dumbbell back down to the shoulder (just like you would during a shoulder press), before taking it back to the floor.

9. Once the dumbbell touches the floor, continue with successive reps. You can use the same hand to complete the programmed reps, or change hands between each rep.

10. If done with heavier loads, see every rep as a single, perfectly performed movement.

11. Depending on the weight being used, complete 3-5 sets of 5-20 reps on each side.

Chapter Five: Core

What is your core?

Your core is the musculature of your torso. These muscles are responsible for both stabilisation and the transfer of force from one aspect of movement to the next, for example changing direction. Core stability is often referred to as *trunk stability*.

It makes sense for your body's centre of mass and the areas directly surrounding it to require the strength to support the movement of your limbs. A lack of core muscular development can result in a loss of performance and a predisposition to injury.

Integral components of your core include the pelvic floor, diaphragm, transversus abdominis and the multifidus. These make a cylinder which facilitates intra-abdominal pressure, which is explained below.

The Transverse Abdominis

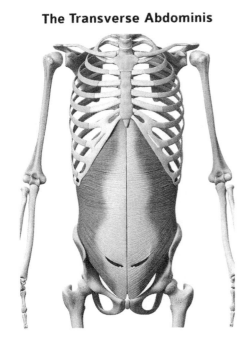

The Rectus Abdominis

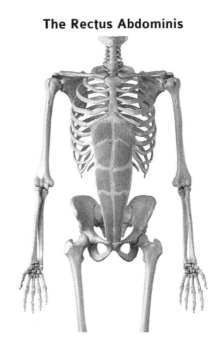

However, the rectus abdominis (abs) and the external and internal obliques are the most renowned aspects of your core as they are so associated with your superficial physique.

Other muscles integral to trunk stability, but not so commonly associated as *core*, are the erector spinae, lats and glutes.

When you engage the core musculature, it's referred to as *bracing your core*. As the musculature that surrounds your midsection contracts, it creates a brace that provides support.

The support provided by the bracing of the muscles is reinforced with the *Valsalva manoeuvre* which is a moderately forceful attempted exhalation against a closed airway. Like equalizing your ears on an airplane and blowing against a pinched nose.

The contraction of the core muscles and the held breath creates *intra-abdominal pressure* (IAP), and this increased pressure in the abdomen greatly increases the stability of the spine and maximises performance when lifting heavy loads.

How do you develop your core?

One of the best ways to train your core is to ensure you brace the core properly (imagine someone is about to punch you in the stomach) during the many strength and power exercises described throughout this book. From there, specific development of the core should be worked.

When starting with a new client, I always ensure we begin by developing their ability to resist bending, extending and rotational forces on their spine. From there, we work towards incorporating these movements.

In this chapter, I have included six exercises that are integral for the development of optimal core stability.

RKC Plank

Plank variations are isometric holds where your core musculature works to resist gravity as it pushes you into *hyperextension* and *lateral flexion* (side bending) of your spine.

The RKC plank is named after the Russian Kettlebell Challenge by Pavel Tsatsouline, a famous Russian strength coach. It uses a few slight variations from the standard front plank, while concentrating on engaging total body tension.

The RKC plank has been shown to get four times the ab engagement of the conventional front plank and is my plank variation of choice.

You don't need to hold the RKC for minutes at a time. If you contract your core maximally, short rounds with even shorter rest periods work perfectly.

Often coaches will state that, "If you can plank for a minute with ease, then you need to progress the exercise." I am sure this is true for planks where there is little to no conscious engagement, but if you maximally engage the associated musculature, even 20-30 seconds will be enough for most people.

1. Kneel on the floor and clasp your hands together so that your forearms are at a 45-degree angle.

2. Place your forearms onto the floor just as you would during a standard front plank. To increase the intensity, place your arms further forward, so that your elbows sit in front of your shoulders.

3. Step back with your left then right foot at hip to shoulder width.

4. Maximally contract your glutes and abs, which will tilt your pelvis back slightly.

5. Maximally contract your quads and core musculature. Pull back with your forearms (as if you are pulling your elbows towards your toes) to increase your core engagement.

6. Complete 3-5 sets of 30-40 seconds.

Side Planks

The side plank is an underused exercise that's ideal for the development and maintenance of the core musculature that supports your spine and resists *lateral flexion* (side bending of the spine), specifically the obliques and the quadratus lumborum.

1. Lie on your right-hand side and place your right forearm onto the floor, perpendicular to your body.

2. Placing your left foot on the front of your right foot helps to keep your hips in a balanced position and allows you to easily transition between front and side plank variations.

3. Raise your hips so there is no side bending of your spine and so that your lower legs are raised off the floor.

4. Engage your glutes, so your hips are extended. Having slightly bent hips is a common fault.

5. Maximally brace your core musculature, as you would during an RKC plank.

6. Either keep your left arm flat to your body or raise it to the sky.

7. Complete 2-3 sets of 30-40 seconds on each side.

Pallof Iso Hold

This exercise is usually performed as a *pallof press* where you press the resistance band rather than sustaining an isometric hold (no movement). However, the pallof iso hold is my favourite anti-rotation exercise.

The pallof isometric hold can be performed in various stances while standing or kneeling. These variations should be practised as they help to build lumbo-pelvic (lumbar spine and pelvis) stability in different positions.

1. Use a red band. The tension can be varied by standing closer to, or further away from the band attachment point if required.

2. Attach the band to something solid at chest height, looping the band through itself.

3. Grasp the band with both hands and stand side-on to the attachment point, holding your hands at your chest.

4. Sidestep away from the attachment point to add tension to the band.

5. Ensure that your feet, hips and shoulders are forward facing. Don't counter the band tension by turning away from the attachment point.

6. For an isometric hold, press the band out and hold it for 30-40 seconds.

7. If performing the pallof press, engage your core and press the band to your front, holding it for 2-5 seconds, before returning it to the starting position and proceeding with successive reps.

8. Complete 2-3 sets of 30-40 seconds or 5-15 reps on each side.

McGill Curl Ups

McGill curl ups are named after Dr Stuart McGill. He is a leading spinal researcher who promotes the use of what he calls "The Big Three". These are McGill curl ups, birddogs and side planks. They are his non-negotiable core exercises for a healthy lower spine.

McGill curl ups are essentially a sit up variation, which work your abs without excessively flexing your lumbar vertebrae.

The exercise may look easy, but as with all core work, when performed correctly by consciously engaging the muscles you are targeting, they are one of the toughest ab exercises out there. They also strengthen the neck, which is an added bonus for fighters.

1. Lie down with your head flat on the floor.

2. Bend your left leg, bringing your heel up towards your glutes, while keeping your right leg extended.

3. Bend your elbows and place your hands under your lower back. This ensures you maintain a neutral spine throughout the movement. Keeping your elbows raised off the floor throughout the movement makes it harder.

4. Slowly raise your head and shoulders up a few inches and maximally contract your abs for 10 seconds before slowly returning to the starting position.

5. Try not to roll your chin towards your chest. Keep your chin retracted as you raise your shoulders and head up.

6. Complete 3-5 sets of 5 reps with 10 second pauses at the top.

Ab Roll Outs

Ab roll-outs work your abs incredibly hard while requiring you to maintain the posture of your lumbo-pelvic region, making them one of the best core exercises in your arsenal.

The need to maintain a neutral pelvis and lower spine position while bending and extending your hips and knees makes the ab roll-out not only a great exercise for your abs, but also the ideal core exercise to ingrain proper function while squatting.

Caution must be practised with the ab roll-out as form can easily be lost, causing the lower back to dip and in some cases resulting in strains in the abs.

Many of your adductors connect to your pubis on your pelvis, which is the same area that your abdominals attach. Therefore, combining the engagement of these muscles will increase your overall stability during the exercise.

To increase adductor engagement during the roll-out, simply place a medicine ball between your legs and squeeze your legs together as you roll out.

You can use an ab roller or even the plates on a barbell.

1. Kneel with your hips stacked over your knees and grab the roller/barbell.

2. Take a big gulp of air, brace your core and use the Valsalva manoeuvre.

3. Slowly roll the roller out to the front and allow your body to extend. Ensure your lower spine doesn't dip.

4. Once your hips are fully extended, or you have reached the furthest point your core strength allows, slowly return to the starting position and exhale.

5. Complete 3-5 sets of 5-10 reps. (Pauses can be used at the bottom; be careful if using the Valsalva manoeuvre).

Landmine Rotations

Most conventional exercises involve using forwards, rearwards and lateral movement, to take the body from point A to point B and usually back to A.

However, the use of rotational movement is becoming all-pervading with many trainers, as they deem this style of *functional training* to be key to human movement and longevity.

Unfortunately, this ideology of functionality is often taken to an extreme. Entire training regimes are programmed around rotational complexes (a complex being a series of movements or exercises combined).

Although these movements can look impressive, they simply don't achieve the level of physical improvement that variations of the hinge, squat, push and pull can. However, the safe development of rotational strength should be practised, and landmine rotations are an effective way of doing this.

The landmine rotation closely mimics the mechanics of a strike, in that it requires you to pivot your feet, rotate and extend your hips, and transfer the force produced in your legs into your upper body.

1. Place the barbell in a landmine with plates. 45cm plates can be used but small 5-10kg plates are optimal, as large plates can get in the way.

2. Stand on the left side of the barbell, facing it in a slit stance, with your right leg in front of your left, and your toes forward facing.

3. Take an underhand grip of the barbell with your right hand at the top of the sleeve.

4. Take an overhand grip with your left hand next to your right hand.

5. Pick the barbell up, maintaining a slight bend in the hips and knees so that the barbell sits at your mid-lower thigh.

6. Pivot on your feet and rotate with your hips to bring the barbell across to your left thigh. There will also be some rotation in your thoracic spine.

7. To maximally engage the double pulse, create total body tension before rotating from your right thigh. As the barbell rotates round, allow for tension to release to maximise speed. Once the barbell comes to your left thigh, facilitate a secondary contraction which creates total body tension and decelerates the barbell (ensuring you don't strike your thigh).

8. Quickly return the barbell back to the starting position on your right thigh before completing successive reps.

9. Depending on the weight being use, complete 3-5 sets of 4-20 reps – each rotation counting as 1 rep.

Chapter Six: Neck Strength

Neck strength is extremely important for fighters. This is due to the neck's role in resisting forces that act to suddenly change the direction of the head i.e. making a strike or dodging a blow.

When a strike causes a sudden movement of the head it can result in a concussion (a traumatic brain injury). An even bigger problem is what's referred to as *second impact syndrome*, where a second concussion occurs before the brain is fully recovered from the first. When this happens, the brain can swell rapidly, which results in a greater risk of long term issues.

It's the muscles of your neck that transfer the force (from a strike) from your head into your torso, ultimately helping to protect you from a head injury so it is essential to train these muscles.

When it comes to neck training, caution must be taken as the vertebrae that make up the neck are not surrounded by other skeletal structures or numerous large muscle groups that help support the area. If you treat neck training as you would leg training, for example, there is a high potential for severe injury.

Just as with the core, the primary functions you are trying to build are stabilisation and the ability to resist forces. For this reason, I always start neck training with upper back work and anti-movements (resisting movement), before moving onto exercises that isolate neck movements, such as neck curls. These will help you develop huge neck strength, but I recommend you first build a base of strength in your neck with shrugs and banded neck iso holds.

The deep muscles on the back of the neck

The Levator Scapula

The Trapezius

The muscles on the front of your neck

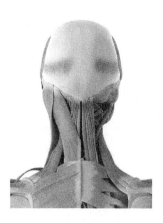

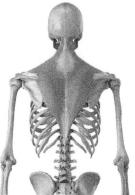

Shrugs

When it comes to neck training, I like to work from the shoulders up, initially working the large upper back muscle (traps) that connects onto the back of your head.

It is safe to load the traps heavy and they can be effectively trained to help support your neck. Working heavy shrugging movements will also result in engagement from the surrounding neck muscles, reinforcing the benefits.

Dumbbells can be used effectively for shrugs, but if you have access to a hex bar, I would recommend using it as it places your hands away from your sides and allows you to lift heavier loads.

1. Stand upright in good posture with a dumbbell in each hand at your sides or use a hex bar.

2. Brace your core.

3. Without bending your elbows shrug your shoulders upwards as high as you can. Don't work in a circular motion, simply up and down.

4. Ensure your shoulders are driving upwards and you are not driving your head and back downwards.

5. It often works better to inhale during the upwards phase of the lift rather than during the downward phase (this is the opposite to most strength exercises) – its feels more natural to have your ribcage expanding as you shrug your shoulders.

6. Hold the top position for a second or two before slowly lowering the dumbbells/hex bar back down to the starting position and complete successive reps.

7. Complete 3-5 sets of 10-20 reps.

Banded Neck Iso Holds

Banded neck iso holds are one of my favourite neck strengthening exercises as they work the neck hard, while reducing many of the risks of flexing and extending the neck under load.

1. Use a red band. The tension can be varied by standing closer or further away from the band attachment point.

2. Attach the band to a solid structure at head height.

3. Wrap a small towel around the part of the band which goes around your head as the rubber band can pull on your hair.

4. Place the band around your head (above your ears) and step away from the attachment point to add tension to the band.

5. You can stand facing the band attachment point, with your back to it, with your right or left side facing it, or at an oblique angle from the band attachment point to work the different areas of the neck.

6. Ensure that your feet, hips, shoulders and head are forward facing. Don't counter the band tension by turning away from the attachment point.

7. Engage your core, create tension in your upper back and neck and hold the position for 30-40 seconds.

8. Complete 1-3 sets of 30-40 seconds in each position.

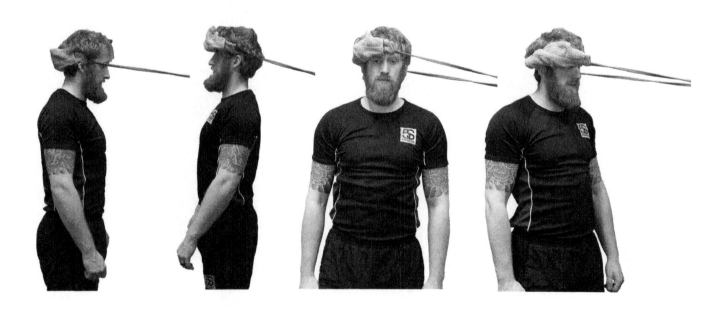

Neck Curls

Neck curls are an effective neck strengthening exercise, but extra care must be taken not to stress the vertebrae and intervertebral discs.

Neck curls can be performed using the weight of your own head, flexing and extending your neck while it is hanging off a bench. However, wrapping weight plates in a towel, resting them on your head, and maintaining support with your hands is an effective way to load the exercise.

Although doing this looks a little ridiculous, when done properly, it will result in huge increases in neck strength.

Neck curls can be done face up, face down and with you facing each direction (on your side). Always warm up with unloaded reps first and progress the weight slowly. Don't overload the exercise; if you concentrate on feeling the muscles working (mind muscle connection), a moderate load will be sufficient.

On your back:

1. Lie on your back on a bench with your head completely hanging off the end. Isometric holds can be done in this position.

2. Lower your head back under control before flexing your head back up to, and slightly beyond, the starting position.

3. If using a plate with a towel as a cushion, place the plate on your forehead and support it with your hands.

4. Complete 3-5 sets of 5-10 reps.

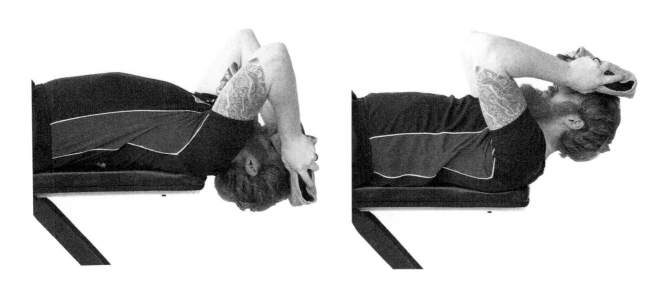

On your front:

1. Lie on your front on a bench with your head completely hanging off the end. Isometric holds can be done in this position.

2. Lower your head forward under control before extending your head back up to and slightly beyond the starting position.

3. If using a plate with a towel as a cushion, place the plate on the upper part of the back of your head (crown) and support it with your hands.

4. Complete 3-5 sets of 5-10 reps.

On your sides:

1. Lie on your left or right side on a bench with your head completely hanging off the end. Isometric holds can be done in this position.

5. Lower your head down to the side under control before extending your head back up to and slightly beyond the starting position.

2. If using a plate with a towel as a cushion, place the plate on the upper part of the side of your head (above your ear) and support it with your hands.

3. Complete 3-5 sets of 5-10 reps.

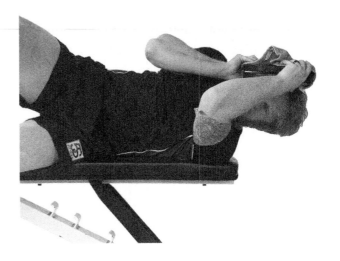

Chapter Seven: Programming

When programming, the easiest way to test strength is with a *one repetition maximum lift* or 1RM. This is the absolute maximum you can lift for one repetition (a *training max* is a 1RM with no breakdown in form, which is what I work off). We then work off percentages of the 1RM to quantify the programme.

Testing a 1RM can be quite stressful on the athlete and comes with a certain risk of injury, especially if the athlete is not an experienced lifter.

Due to this risk, coaches also work off an athlete's 2, 3, and 5RM, which are all much less stressful to test. To estimate your 1RM from your 2, 3, or 5RM, we use formulas or coefficients (although 1RM apps can be downloaded to your phone).

A coefficient is a constant number that is multiplied by the variable (weight lifted). These coefficients have been worked out over various studies and are surprisingly accurate.

The coefficient for a 5RM is 1.16. If your 5RM is 100kg, for instance, multiply that weight by 1.16 to find your 1RM. In this case, the 1RM would be 116kg.

Different coefficients and formulas give negligibly different results, but they all work well as estimations from which to programme.

During the basic development of strength, I have my athletes work at between 70% – 85% of their 1RM, and during dynamic effort sets (lifting with high acceleration and speed) I have them work at between 50% – 60% of their 1RM

Another method to quantify your programming is the *rating of perceived exertion* (RPE) scale. This is simply a scale which rates your perceived level of physical effort. The simplest scale is a 1-10 rating with 1 being almost no exertion, 5 being moderate exertion, and 10 being the hardest it could possibly be for the number of reps programmed.

Both 1RM percentages and the RPE scale are used in the example program.

Rest Periods

The main purpose of rest periods is to allow your breathing and heart rate to reduce. This allows substances that may impede training intensity to clear, while allowing substances that provide energy to be restored.

Another important aspect of rest is to allow time for your nervous system to recover. This is especially important in strength training, specifically when working at maximal loads.

As a fighter, you are probably used to taking as little rest as possible to try and improve overall fitness levels and recovery times. However, when strength training, you need to take sufficient rest periods to allow you to facilitate optimal work on each set – without taking so long that the fatigue from previous sets has completely worn off. In other words, successive sets should have a cumulative effect.

Recommended rest periods:

- When working above 85% of your 1RM, take 3-5 minutes rest between sets.

- When working between 70-85%, take 2-3 minutes rest between sets.

- When working below 70%, take 1-2 minutes rest between sets. However, anywhere up to 3 minutes on assistance work is fine, if needed. Rest periods can be dynamic, depending on how you feel.

- When performing dynamic effort sets, take 40-60 seconds rest between sets.

- Core work is best performed with short rest periods of between 10-30 seconds.

When it comes to heavy strength work, if you need an extra 30 seconds between sets, take it. A better quality set is better than a shorter rest period. We are talking about strength training, not the conditioning of the cardio-respiratory system.

The Program

In this program, you will be working off two sessions a week over an 8-week cycle.

I have programmed in the assistance, core and neck work for the first four weeks. You can carry on with a similar layout in the final 4 weeks. However, I recommend you select exercises that are specific to your needs. In other words, train your weaknesses.

Feel free to cycle squat, deadlift and press variations as you choose. If you like to pull with a sumo stance (video demonstration available), you can cycle it in or use it as your primary lift.

If you do not have access to a landmine attachment, substitute its use with other *push* assistance exercises, such as the dumbbell clean and press or even the dumbbell snatch.

Don't waste too much time and energy on long warm-up sessions prior to resistance training (I have programmed warm up drills on the first 4 weeks). Warming up with light sets of the primary movement or similar assistance exercise is usually sufficient. However, I do recommend working with the RAMP warmup protocol:

- **R**aise – heart rate and body temperature. This could be as simple as high knees or bodyweight squats. However, ideally you want the movements to be specific to the exercises you will perform.

- **A**ctivate – key muscle groups you are using during the session i.e. an RDL with a conscious engagement of the glutes (squeeze them hard at the top) could be used as a glute activation drill prior to deadlifting.

- **M**obilise – joints. You don't want to spend hours mobilising your whole body. Concentrate on areas that might limit your ability to perform a movement effectively. For example, mobilising areas that limit your ability to achieve a deep squat or stretching your hip flexors prior to deadlifting allows you to facilitate stronger hip extension.

- **P**otentiate – prime the body for maximal intensity i.e. progressively load the weight.

An example of progressively loading up for the back squat for 5x5 could be:

- 1-2 Sets with an unloaded barbell (5-10 Reps).

- 1 Set at 60% of the maximum weight you will be working at (5-10 Reps).

- 1 Set at 80% of the maximum weight you will be working at (5 Reps).

- Begin your first set of the programmed weight.

For this program, find out your 1RMs using the techniques in the introduction of this chapter (test your 1RM or estimate it from your 5RM). From there, work off the programmed percentages, but allow yourself 5% either side to allow leeway for good and bad days.

This program can be repeated. Simply increase the weight used progressively. After 8 weeks, retest your 1RMs and work off these new numbers. As you gain experience, add in new assistance exercises when necessary.

Finish the following program 1-2 weeks before a fight, to allow time to taper. This does not necessarily mean ceasing all resistance training, but volume (how many sets and reps), intensity (how heavy), and possibly frequency (how often), should be tapered.

Protocol – Primary Lifts:

All percentages are based off training maxes with no breakdown in your form.

If available, use accommodating resistance on dynamic effort sets (see the Accommodating Resistance section to recap on how to set up bands on the barbell).

If accommodating resistance is not available, simply lift with maximal speed at the programmed percentage (+10-15% on squats and deadlifts, and +5-10% on presses) and use compensatory acceleration.

Work 1-2 assistance exercises and 2-3 core/neck exercises each session, depending on how you feel.

Week 1: 5x5 at 75%

Week 2: 5x5 at 75-80%

Week 3: 5x3 at 80-85%

Week 4: 5x2 at 90%

Week 5, 6 & 7: 3x3 at 80-85% / 10x2 (Squat & Pull) 8x3 (Push) at 60% +Bands Dynamic Effort

Week 8: 12x2 (Squat & Pull) 10x3 (Push) at 50-60% +Bands Dynamic Effort

Weeks 5, 6 and 7 take advantage of *postactivation potentiation* (PAP), which refers to the increase of strength in nerve pathways that have been used previously. In layman's terms, this means that the associated muscles are primed and working at full capacity. Lighter loads often feel abnormally light after working with heavier loads.

Week 1 – Session 1

Warm Up/Activation/Prehab:

Exercise	Sets/Reps (% / RPE)	Rest	Notes
Goblet Squat	2x10 - RPE 6	20-30 Seconds	
Band Pull Apart & External Rotations	2x10 Each exercise	15-20 Seconds	

Primary:

Exercise	Sets/Reps (% / RPE)	Rest	Notes
Back Squat	5x5 - 75%	2-3 Minutes	
Overhead Press	5x5 - 75%	2-3 Minutes	

Assistance:

Exercise	Sets/Reps (% / RPE)	Rest	Notes
Landmine Single Arm Press	4x10 Each side - RPE 8	60-90 Seconds	

Core & Neck:

Exercise	Sets/Reps/Time	Rest	Notes
Landmine Rotations	3x20 @RPE 7	30-60 Seconds	
Pallof Iso Hold	3x30 Seconds - each side	20-30 Seconds	
Banded Neck Iso Holds	2x30 Seconds - each side	15-20 Seconds	

Week 1 – Session 2

Warm Up/Activation/Prehab:

Exercise	Sets/Reps (% / RPE)	Rest	Notes
Band Face Pulls	3x10 - RPE 6	20-30 Seconds	
RDL's	2x10 - RPE 5	30 Seconds	

Primary:

Exercise	Sets/Reps (% / RPE)	Rest	Notes
Deadlift	5x5 - 75%	2-3 Minutes	
Bench Press	5x5 - 75%	2-3 Minutes	

Assistance:

Exercise	Sets/Reps (% / RPE)	Rest	Notes
Single Arm Rows	4x10 Each side - RPE 8	60-90 Seconds	

Core & Neck:

Exercise	Sets/Reps/Time	Rest	Notes
Shrugs	3x10 - RPE 7	30-60 Seconds	
Ab Roll Outs	3x10	20-30 Seconds	
RKC Plank	3x30 Seconds	15-20 Seconds	

Week 2 – Session 1

Warm Up/Activation/Prehab:

Exercise	Sets/Reps (% / RPE)	Rest	Notes
Goblet Squat	2x10 - RPE 6	20-30 Seconds	
Band Pull Apart & External Rotations	2x10 Each exercise	15-20 Seconds	

Primary:

Exercise	Sets/Reps (% / RPE)	Rest	Notes
Front Squat	5x5 - 75-80%	2-3 Minutes	
Push Press	5x5 - 75-80%	2-3 Minutes	

Assistance:

Exercise	Sets/Reps (% / RPE)	Rest	Notes
Power Clean	5x3 - RPE 8	60-90 Seconds	

Core & Neck:

Exercise	Sets/Reps/Time	Rest	Notes
McGill Curl Ups	3x5 – 10 Second pause at top	30-60 Seconds	
Side Planks	3x30 Seconds - each side	20-30 Seconds	
Neck Curls	2x10 Each side	15-20 Seconds	

Week 2 – Session 2

Warm Up/Activation/Prehab:

Exercise	Sets/Reps (% / RPE)	Rest	Notes
Band Face Pulls	3x10 - RPE 6	20-30 Seconds	
RDL's	2x10 - RPE 5	30 Seconds	

Primary:

Exercise	Sets/Reps (% / RPE)	Rest	Notes
Hex Bar Deadlift	5x5 - 75-80%	2-3 Minutes	
Floor Press	5x5 - 75-80%	2-3 Minutes	

Assistance:

Exercise	Sets/Reps (% / RPE)	Rest	Notes
Dumbbell Snatch	4x10 Each side - RPE 8	60-90 Seconds	

Core & Neck:

Exercise	Sets/Reps/Time	Rest	Notes
Shrugs	3x10 - RPE 7	30-60 Seconds	
Landmine Rotations	3x20 - RPE 7	30-60 Seconds	
Pallof Iso Hold	3x30 Seconds – each side	20-30 Seconds	

Week 3 – Session 1

Warm Up/Activation/Prehab:

Exercise	Sets/Reps (% / RPE)	Rest	Notes
Goblet Squat	2x10 - RPE 6	20-30 Seconds	
Band Pull Apart & External Rotations	2x10 Each exercise	15-20 Seconds	

Primary:

Exercise	Sets/Reps (% / RPE)	Rest	Notes
Back Squat	5x3 – 80-85%	2-3 Minutes	
Overhead Press	5x3 – 80-85%	2-3 Minutes	

Assistance:

Exercise	Sets/Reps (% / RPE)	Rest	Notes
Landmine Split Jerk	4x5 Each side - RPE 8	60-90 Seconds	

Core & Neck:

Exercise	Sets/Reps/Time	Rest	Notes
Landmine Rotations	3x20 - RPE 7	30-60 Seconds	
Pallof Iso Hold	3x30 Seconds - each side	20-30 Seconds	
Neck Curls	2x10 Each side	15-20 Seconds	

Week 3 – Session 2

Warm Up/Activation/Prehab:

Exercise	Sets/Reps (% / RPE)	Rest	Notes
Band Face Pulls	3x10 - RPE 6	20-30 Seconds	
RDL's	2x10 - RPE 5	30 Seconds	

Primary:

Exercise	Sets/Reps (% / RPE)	Rest	Notes
Deadlift	5x3 - 80-85%	2-3 Minutes	
Bench Press	5x3 - 80-85%	2-3 Minutes	

Assistance:

Exercise	Sets/Reps (% / RPE)	Rest	Notes
RDL's	4x8 - RPE 8	60-90 Seconds	
KB Swings	3x10 - RPE 8	60-90 Seconds	

Core & Neck:

Exercise	Sets/Reps/Time	Rest	Notes
Shrugs	3x10 - RPE 7	30-60 Seconds	
McGill Curl Ups	3x5 – 10 Second pause at top	30-60 Seconds	
Side Planks	3x30 Seconds - each side	20-30 Seconds	

Week 4 – Session 1

Warm Up/Activation/Prehab:

Exercise	Sets/Reps (% / RPE)	Rest	Notes
Goblet Squat	2x10 - RPE 6	20-30 Seconds	
Band Pull Apart & External Rotations	2x10 Each exercise	15-20 Seconds	

Primary:

Exercise	Sets/Reps (% / RPE)	Rest	Notes
Front Squat	5x2 - 90%	3-5 Minutes	
Push Press	5x2 - 90%	3-5 Minutes	

Assistance:

Exercise	Sets/Reps (% / RPE)	Rest	Notes
Power Clean	5x3 - RPE 8	60-90 Seconds	
Landmine Split Jerk	4x3 Each side - RPE 8	60-90 Seconds	

Core & Neck:

Exercise	Sets/Reps/Time	Rest	Notes
Landmine Rotations	3x20 - RPE 7	30-60 Seconds	
Pallof Iso Hold	3x30 Seconds – each side	20-30 Seconds	
Neck Curls	2x10 Each side	15-20 Seconds	

Week 4 – Session 2

Warm Up/Activation/Prehab:

Exercise	Sets/Reps (% / RPE)	Rest	Notes
Band Face Pulls	3x10 - RPE 6	20-30 Seconds	
RDL's	2x10 - RPE 5	30 Seconds	

Primary:

Exercise	Sets/Reps (% / RPE)	Rest	Notes
Hex Bar Deadlift	5x2 - 90%	3-5 Minutes	
Floor Press	5x2 - 90%	3-5 Minutes	

Assistance:

Exercise	Sets/Reps (% / RPE)	Rest	Notes
Rack Pulls	4x5 - RPE 8	60-90 Seconds	
Dumbbell Snatch	4x10 Each side - RPE 8	60-90 Seconds	

Core & Neck:

Exercise	Sets/Reps/Time	Rest	Notes
Ab Roll Outs	3x10	20-30 Seconds	
RKC Plank	3x30 Seconds	15-20 Seconds	
Banded Neck Iso Holds	2x30 Seconds - each side	15-20 Seconds	

Week 5, 6 & 7 – Session 1:

Choose own assistance, core and neck work. Target weaknesses.

Primary:

Exercise	Sets/Reps (% / RPE)	Rest	Notes
Back Squat or Front Squat	3x3 - 80-85%	2-3 Minutes	
Back Squat or Front Squat	10x2 - 60% +Bands - Dynamic Effort	1 Minute	
Overhead Press or Push Press	3x3 – 80-85%	2-3 Minutes	
Overhead Press or Push Press	8x3 - 60% +Bands - Dynamic Effort	1 Minute	

Week 5, 6 & 7 – Session 2:

Choose own assistance, core and neck work. Target weaknesses.

Exercise	Sets/Reps (% / RPE)	Rest	Notes
Conventional, Sumo or Hex Bar Deadlift	3x3 - 80-85%	2-3 Minutes	
Hex Bar Jumps	10x2 - 60% +Bands - Dynamic Effort	1 Minute	
Bench Press or Floor Press	3x3 - 80-85%	2-3 Minutes	
Bench Press or Floor Press	8x3 - 60% +Bands - Dynamic Effort	1 Minute	

Week 8 – Session 1:

Choose own assistance, core and neck work. Target weaknesses.

Exercise	Sets/Reps (% / RPE)	Rest	Notes
Back Squat or Front Squat	12x2 – 50-60% +Bands - Dynamic Effort	1 Minute	
Overhead Press or Push Press	10x3 – 50-60% - Dynamic Effort	1 Minute	

Week 8 – Session 2:

Choose own assistance, core and neck work. Target weaknesses.

Exercise	Sets/Reps (% / RPE)	Rest	Notes
Hex Bar Jumps	12x2 – 50-60% +Bands - Dynamic Effort	1 Minute	
Bench Press or Floor Press	10x3 – 50-60% +Bands - Dynamic Effort	1 Minute	

Glossary of Terms and Equipment

Anatomical Term	Definition/Description
Abdominals Rectus Abdominis / Obliques	Muscles on the front of the abdomen – rectus abdominis (6 pack muscles) / obliques (muscles to the side of the rectus abdominis).
Achilles Tendon	Tendon on the back of the heel.
Adductors	Muscles on the inner side of the thighs.
Calves Gastrocnemius / Soleus	Muscles on the rear of the lower leg.
Core Musculature	The musculature of your torso, but more specifically it is the lumbo-pelvic region (lumbar spine and pelvis, often referred to as your 'lower back'). These muscles are responsible for both stabilisation and the transfer of force from one of movement to the next, for example changing direction.
Deltoid (delts)	Shoulder muscles – anterior delts (front section) / medial delts (middle section) / posterior delts (rear section).
Diaphragm	A dome shaped muscle used in respiration.
Erector Spinae	Muscles that run up either side of the spine
Gluteals (Glutes) Maximus / Medius / Minor	The buttock muscles – major (largest muscle) / medius (middle muscle) / minor (smallest muscle). The gluteal muscles along with the TFL are also referred to as the hip abductors.
Hamstrings Biceps Femoris / Semimembranosus / Semitendinosus	The three muscles on the rear side of the upper leg
Hip Flexors Psoas Major / Iliacus	The muscles on the front of the hips.
Iliotibial Band (ITB)	A band of connective tissue that runs down the outer side of the thigh.
Latissimus Dorsi (Lats)	Mid- back muscle.
Ligaments	A short band of tough, flexible fibrous connective tissue which connects two bones, and helps to hold a joint together.
Muscle Insertion	The insertion is where the muscle ends and is the point at which the muscle is attached to the bone moved by that muscle.
Muscle Origin	The origin is the start of a muscle and is attached to the fixed bone, which is the one which doesn't move during the contraction.
Pectoralis (Pecs) Major / Minor	Chest muscles – major (larger muscle) / minor (smaller muscle)
Peroneals Peroneus Longus / Peroneus Brevis	Muscles on the outer side of the lower legs.
Piriformis	Small muscle underneath the gluteus maximus.
Plantar Fascia	Thick band of connective tissue on the sole of the foot.

Quadratus Lumbo- rum (QL)	Muscles on either side of the lower back.
Quadriceps (Quads) Rectus Femoris / Vastus Medialis / Vastus Intermedius / Vastus Lateralis	The four muscles of the thigh.
Rhomboids	Upper back muscles between the shoulder blades.
Sciatic Nerve	A major nerve extending from the lower end of the spinal cord, through the glutes and down the back of the thigh.
Tendons	A flexible but inelastic cord of strong fibrous collagen tissue attaching a muscle to a bone.
Tensor Fasciae Latae (TFL)	Muscle on the upper outer side of the thigh.
Thoracic Spine	The thoracic spine is the twelve vertebrae between the base of your neck and the bottom of your rib cage. Often when we refer to the thoracic spine in a training environment, we are referring to the muscles which surround it.
Transverse Abdomi- nis (TVA)	The deepest muscle of the abdominal wall and is an integral component of the core
Trapezius (Traps)	Upper back muscle.

Technical Term	Definition/Description
1 Rep Max (1RM)	Most you can lift for 1 rep. I usually work off *Training Maxes*, meaning there is no breakdown in form.
Abduction	Moving limbs back in towards the midline from a lateral position.
Activation	Getting a specific muscle working.
Adduction	Moving a limb laterally away from the midline.
Agonist	The muscle performing the action – the biceps during a biceps curl.
Anatomical Breathing	Synchronizing your breathing with your movements
Antagonist	The muscles that produce an opposing joint torque to the agonist muscles – the triceps during a biceps curl.
Anterior	Front of the body.
Anterior Pelvic Tilt	Pelvis that tilts excessively forward.
Anti-Extension	Resisting forces that try to extend your spine.
Anti-flexion/Lateral Flexion	Resisting forces that try to flex or laterally-flex your spine.
Anti-Rotation	Resisting forces that try to rotate your spine.
Assistance Lifts	Often referred to as *accessory exercises* are also compound movements. They are chosen to develop specific movements or muscle groups that help you to perform the primary lift or specific sporting actions.
Auxiliary Lifts	These single joint exercises. They are chosen to help develop your ability to perform the primary lift or specific sporting actions.
Ballistic	Refers to movements that exhibit maximum acceleration and velocity over short periods of time. Essentially both the concentric (upwards) and eccentric (downwards) phases of this lift are completed with good speed.
Bilateral	Working both sides of the body at the same time.
Biomechanical breathing	Breathing in before or during the eccentric phase, and breathing out during the later stages or after the concentric phase. This method increases total body tension.
Cadence	Stride frequency – the number of strides a runner takes in a minute.
Cervical Spine	Neck – should have a normal lordotic/inwards curve (lordosis).
Compound Exercises/ Movements	Exercises which include multiple joints and muscle groups.
Concentric Phase/Contraction	The upwards phase of a movement, where the muscle(s) are shortening under tension.
Delayed Onset Muscle Soreness (DOMS)	The muscle soreness you feel days after a workout.
Diaphragmatic Breathing	Effectively using the diaphragm during respiration.
Dorsi-Flexion	Refers to flexion at your ankle so that your toes are pointing upwards
Dynamic Effort Method	Lifting at speed – Working between 50-60% of 1RM.
Eccentric Phase/Contraction	The downwards phase of a movement, where the muscle(s) are lengthening under tension.
Extension	when the angle between the two bones increases – straightening a joint.

Fixators & Neutralizers	These muscles help to stabilize the movement.
Flexibility	This refers to a range of motion a muscle can achieve passively, essentially the length it can achieve.
Flexion	When the angle decreases between the two bones attached to either side of the joint being affected – bending a joint.
Foot Strike	The way the foot lands while running.
Golgi Tendon Organ	Receptor organ that senses changes in muscle tension. It can tell muscles to *shut off* when stimulated.
Intra-abdominal Pressure (IAP)	Increased pressure in the abdomen caused by a held breath and contraction of the core muscles.
Isometric Contraction	A muscle contraction where there is no change in muscle length
Lateral-Flexion	Side bending of the spine.
Low Back Pain	Pain, muscle tension, or stiffness localized below the costal margin (bottom rib) and above the inferior gluteal folds (bottom of your buttocks), with or without sciatica.
Lumbar Spine	Lower back – should have a normal lordotic/inwards curve (lordosis).
Lumbo-Pelvic Region	The lumbar spine and pelvis.
Maximal Effort Training	Maximal weight. Working above 90% of your 1RM
Midline	Centre line of the body
Mind-Muscle Connection (MMC)	Consciously thinking about the muscle, you are working to increase its engagement.
Mobility	How freely a joint can move throughout its full range of motion actively. Flexibility is one very important aspect of mobility.
Motor Unit	A neuron and the muscle fibres which it contracts.
Muscle Tension	Tension is often considered to be the same as tightness. However, not only tight or overworked muscles become tense. Muscles that are lengthened or weak can also become tense – examples of these will pop up throughout the book.
Muscle Tightness	This refers to the muscle-length. If a muscle is tight, then it is shortened. Some muscles have the tendency to be shorter and tighter, while others have the tendency to be longer and less activated.
Muscular Imbalance	Occurs when opposing muscles provide different directions of tension due to tightness and/or weakness.
Nasal Breathing	Breathing through the nose.
Negative Stress	Physical Stress that is maladaptive and leads to injuries and regressions in physical performance.
Neutral Pelvis	A pelvis which sits in the optimal position.
Neutral Spine	A spine which is unbent and untwisted, with three natural curves.
Over-Pronation	When your soles turn outwards slightly more than what is considered optimal, placing more load onto the inner side of the ball of your foot.
Plantar-Flexion	Refers to extension at your ankle so that your toes point downwards towards the floor.

Positive Stress	Physical stress that is adaptive and leads to improvements in physical performance.
Posterior	Rear of the body.
Posterior Pelvic Tilt	Pelvis that tilts excessively rearwards.
Posture	A position which aligns your body so that minimal stress is placed on joints and the supporting muscles, tendons, and ligaments. This results in the stresses of daily life being distributed evenly.
Potentiate/Post-Activation Potentiation (PAP)	Potentiation in this context refers to the increase of strength in nerve pathways that have been used previously. Which in layman's terms, means that the associated muscles are primed and working at full capacity. We can use PAP to capitalise on an increase in neuromuscular efficiency – lighter loads often feel abnormally light after working with heavier loads.
Primary Lift	These are compound exercises. They are of most importance in terms of exercise selection as they work movements fully and require the most effort. Therefore, they should be trained first.
Primary/Prime Mover	The muscle most responsible for completing an action.
Pronated Grip	Overhand Grip.
Pronation/Eversion of the Foot	This refers to when the weight it shifted to the inner side of the foot (soles facing outwards).
Proprioception	The body's ability to transmit a sense of position, analyze that information and react to it.
Protraction	Forward movements of structures of the body.
RAMP	A warmup protocol – refers to *Raise, Activate, Mobilise, Potentiate*.
Range of Motion (ROM)	The full movement potential of a joint.
Release Techniques/ Myofascial Release	A method of hands-on therapy that you can perform yourself, usually with a foam roller or massage ball.
Repeated Effort Method	Submaximal weight for maximal reps – I usually program between 60-75% for this method.
Reps & Sets	*Reps* (repetitions) define the number of times you complete an exercise, and *sets* refers to how many times you will repeat that exercise for the specified number of reps. For example, 5 sets of 3 reps (5x3 – sets first), with 2 minute's rest between sets.
Retraction	Rearwards movements of structures of the body.
Sacrum & Coccyx	Back of the pelvis.
Secondary & Tertiary Movers.	Terms used to describe muscles which assist the prime mover (2nd and 3rd to). During compound lifts, often muscles that may not be considered the prime mover, might be producing just as much force to complete the action.
Single-Joint Exercises	Exercises which work a single joint to target a specific muscle.
Strength	Strength is your ability to produce force, the more force you can produce to overcome a resistance (usually tested with a single effort), the stronger you are.
Submaximal Effort Training	Submaximal weight for submaximal reps. Working between 70-90% of 1RM – I usually program between 75-85% of 1RM.
Supinated Grip	Underhand Grip.

Supination/Eversion of the Foot	This refers to when the weight is shifted to the outer side of the foot (soles facing inwards).
Synergists	The muscle(s) which assist the prime mover.
Thoracic Spine	Mid-upper back – should have a normal kyphotic/outwards curve (kyphosis).
Total Body Tension	Creating tension throughout the body by contracting muscles, using the valsalva maneuver and capitalizing on intra-abdominal pressure.
Training Density	The work you can do in each amount of time. For example, 5x10 reps in 15 minutes is less density that 10x10 reps in 15 minutes.
Training Frequency	How often you train.
Training Intensity	How hard you train. For example, how heavy you lift, or how fast you run.
Training Volume	How much you do in a session/workout.
Unilateral	Working one side of the body at a time.
Valsalva Maneuver	A moderately forceful attempted exhalation against a closed airway. Like equalizing your ears on an airplane and blowing against a pinched nose.

Equipment	Definition/Description
Barbell	The barbell is a 7ft long straight bar that weighs 20kg (44lb) and can have weight plates attached to either side. Lower weight bars are available in some gyms.
Dumbbells	Dumbbells are a short bar with a weight (*bell*) at each end. Most gyms will have a wide selection of dumbbells in 1-2.5kg (2-5lb) increments.
Foam Roller	A 90cm foam roller is ideal, (30-45cm rollers are also fine). However, if you choose to spend more you can purchase a 'rumble roller' which allows you to get deeper into specific areas.
Kettlebell	A kettlebell is a large cast-iron ball-shaped weight with a single handle known as the *horn*. Kettlebells usually come in 4kg (9lb) increments.
Massage Ball	You can purchase balls designed specifically for massage, or use a lacrosse ball. Golf balls can be used (rolling the sole of the foot), but they're often too small to be truly effective. Peanut-shaped massage balls allow you to work both sides of your back, while avoiding pressure on your spine.
Plyo Box or Fitness Step	Strength & Conditioning gyms will usually have wooden plyo boxes which allow for three heights to be used (20/24/30 inch), and jerk boxes which stack various box heights. Most commercial gyms will have some form of plyo box, or fitness steps.
Resistance Bands	Long resistance bands come in varying colours, which denote the tension of the band. Yellow: Low tension Red: Medium tension (recommended) Black: Medium tension (greater tension than red)
Small Loop Resistance Bands	Small bands are a great tool for hip and shoulder strengthening drills. The colours of these bands denote varying band tension. However, these colours can vary and therefore, I advise buying a set of 4-5 bands of varying tensions.

Printed in Great Britain
by Amazon

38814418R00059